GROKKING THE AZURE FUNDAMENTALS CERTIFICATION

JAVINPAUL @JAVINPAUL

Grokking THE Azure Fundamentals Certification

Table of Content

PART 1

DESCRIBE AZURE COST MANAGEME NT AND SERVICE LEVEL AGREEMEN TS

Support plans

1 A support plan solution that gives you best practice information, health status and notifications, and 24/7 access to billing information at the lowest possible cost

1. Standard plan
2. Developer plan
3. Basic plan
4. Premier plan

Correct Answer: 3

Explanation:

Azure support basic plan is the cheapest among the plans and it comes with some low features compared to other support plans. Those features include Azure Advisor, Azure Monitor, access to billing information through and ability to submit support tickets.

Ref:

- https://azure.microsoft.com/en-us/support/plans/

2. In which Azure support plans can you open a new support request?

1. Premier and Professional Direct only
1. Premier, Professional Direct, and Standard only
2. Premier, Professional Direct, Standard, and Developer only
3. Premier, Professional Direct, Standard, Developer, and Basic

Correct Answer: 3

Explanation:

Premier, Professional Direct, Standard, and Developer only. You can open support cases in the following plans: Premier,

Professional Direct, Standard, and Developer only. You cannot open support cases in the Basic support plan

Ref:

- https://azure.microsoft.com/en-us/support/plans/

3. Which support plan is the lowest cost option to receive 24?7 access to support engineers by phone?

1. Standard
1. Developer
2. Basic
3. Professional Direct
4. Premier plan

Correct Answer: 1

Explanation

The Basic support plan is free so is therefore the cheapest. The Developer support plan is the cheapest paid-for support plan. The order of support plans in terms of cost ranging from the cheapest to most expensive is: Basic, Developer, Standard, Professional Direct, Premier. However, 24/7 access to technical support by email and phone is only available for Standard, Professional Direct, Premier plans.

Ref:

- https://azure.microsoft.com/en-us/support/plans/

4. Your company plans to purchase an Azure subscription. The company's support policy states that the Azure environment must provide an option to access support engineers by phone or email. You need to recommend which support plan meets the support policy requirement.
Solution: Recommend a Basic support plan.
Does this meet the goal?

1. Yes
1. No

Correct Answer: 2

Explanation

The Basic support plan does not have any technical support for engineers. Access to Support Engineers via email or phone is available in the following support plans: Premier, Professional Direct and standard.

Ref:

- https://azure.microsoft.com/en-us/support/plans/

Support ticket

5. Where can one create an Azure support request from?

1. support.microsoft.com
1. the Azure portal
2. the Knowledge Center
3. the Security & Compliance admin center

Correct Answer: 2

You can create an Azure support request from the Help and Support blade in the Azure portal or from the context menu of an Azure resource in the Support + Troubleshooting section.

Ref:

- https://azure.microsoft.com/en-us/support/create-ticket/

Product lifecycle

6. An Azure service is available to all Azure customers when it is in ?

1. Public review
1. private preview
2. development
3. an Enterprise Agreement (EA) subscription

Correct Answer: 1

Explanation

Public Preview means that the service is in public beta and can be tried out by anyone with an Azure subscription. Services in public preview are often offered at a discount price. Public previews are excluded from SLAs and in some cases, no support is offered.

Azure Cost Management

7. Your Company needs to copy 500 GBs of data from Azure storage to local premises. Does this process lead to more charges from Azure?

1. Yes
1. No

Correct Answer: 1

Explanation

All outbound data traffic, also called egress, from azure is charged and only the first 5GB is free. Data transfer also between regions is charged. Data transfer between VMs in the same availability zone is free at the moment

Ref:

- https://azure.microsoft.com/en-us/pricing/details/bandwidth/

8. Which of the following is NOT a recommended action you should take on a Virtual machine that is currently underutilized but still contains some important files you may need in a near future?

1. Deallocate the Virtual Machine
1. Reduce the VM size to the lowest sensible size available
2. Delete the VM
3. Delete the VM?s unused resources that generate charges

Correct Answer: 3

Explanation

When you delete a Virtual Machine it also deletes are the files in it permanently and on this scenario you risk losing all the important filcs you had saved there. The best action is to reduce the VM size, deallocate it and then delete resources that are no longer needed.

Ref:

- https://docs.microsoft.com/en-us/learn/modules/plan-manage-azure-costs/6-manage-minimize-total-cost

9. Which is the most efficient way for your company?s testing team could save costs on virtual machines on weekends, when testers are not at work?

1. Delete the virtual machines before the weekend and create a new set the following week.
1. Deallocate virtual machines when they're not in use.
2. Just let everything run. Azure bills you only for the CPU time that you use.

Correct Answer: 2

Explanation

When you deallocate virtual machines, the associated hard disks and data are still kept in Azure. But you don't pay for CPU or network consumption, which can help save costs.

Ref:

- https://docs.microsoft.com/en-us/learn/modules/plan-manage-azure-costs/6-manage-minimize-total-cost

10. What filter should you use in cost analysis to determine the costs for a specific bill within the billing profile scope?

1. InvoiceID
1. MyInvoice
2. BillID
3. CostID

Correct Answer: 1

Explanation

This filter includes only costs that roll up to the specified invoice ID. To download the invoice and the associated usage details file, select Cost Management +Billing and then select Invoices under Billing on the left pane. Select the required invoice based on the billing period or the invoice ID.

Ref:

- https://docs.microsoft.com/en-us/learn/modules/manage-costs-partner-cost-management/3-reconcile-your-bill

11. Which of the following choices are all the supported budget evaluation periods?

1. Weekly, hourly, and monthly
1. Monthly, quarterly, and annual
2. Monthly and quarterly
3. Annually and hourly

Correct Answer: 2

Explanation

A budget can be created with any of these evaluation periods. Budgets reset automatically at the end of a period (monthly, quarterly, or annually) for the same budget amount when you select an expiration date in the future. Because they reset with the same budget amount, you need to create separate budgets when budgeted currency amounts differ for future periods.

Ref:

- https://docs.microsoft.com/en-us/azure/cost-management-billing/costs/tutorial-acm-create-budgets

12. Which of the following would be considered a technical requirement for your application hosted on Azure that would affect Azure resource costs?

1. The ability for users to cancel orders.
1. The ability for customers to upload and store image files in your application.
2. Sending notifications to procurement when inventory is low.
3. Providing a form for customers to initiate a product return.

Correct Answer: 2

Explanation

This would affect Azure costs, because you would need to account for the storage of images on an Azure service

The more the app usage the more the storage needed to store images in Azure and hence the charges increase.

Ref:

- https://docs.microsoft.com/en-us/learn/modules/azure-well-architected-cost-optimization/2-plan-estimate-costs

13. Your company stores PDF copies of all purchase orders. These files are accessed infrequently after their initial upload, and there is no time criticality associated with their retrieval. Which of the following storage tiers would be the best choice to reduce costs for long-term storage?

1. Hot access tier
1. Cool access tier
2. Archive access tier

Correct Answer: 3

Explanation

This choice is the most cost-effective in the long term.

Azure TCO Calculator

14. What is the Azure TCO calculator?

1. Assists you to calculate your security score on Azure.
1. Helps estimate the cost of Azure AD.
2. Helps you estimate the cost savings of operating your solution on Azure over time, instead of in your on-premises datacenter.
3. Helps you calculate the cost of using different support plans on Azure.

Correct Answer: 3

Explanation

With the TCO Calculator, you enter the details of your on-premises workloads. Then you review the suggested industry average cost (which you can adjust) for related operational costs. These costs include electricity, network maintenance, and IT labor. You're then presented with a side-by-side report. Using the report, you can compare those costs with the same workloads running on Azure.

Ref:

- https://docs.microsoft.com/en-us/learn/modules/plan-manage-azure-costs/2-compare-costs-tco-calculator

Azure Accounts

15. Which of the following are types of Azure subscription provides you with access to Azure resources?

1. Azure Trial
1. Azure public preview
2. Azure Pay-as-go
3. Azure Premium
4. Azure Governance

Correct Answer: 1,4

Explanation

Azure offers both free and paid subscription options to fit your needs and requirements. They are:

- **Free trial:** A free trial subscription provides you with 12 months of popular free services, a credit to explore any Azure service for 30 days, and more than 25 services that are always free.

- **Pay-as-you-go:** A pay-as-you-go subscription enables you to pay for what you use by attaching a credit or debit card to your account

- **Member offers:** Your existing membership to certain Microsoft products and services might provide you with credits for your Azure account and reduced rates on Azure services.

Ref:

- https://docs.microsoft.com/en-us/learn/modules/plan-manage-azure-costs/4-purchase-azure-services

Azure Health Monitoring

16. Azure Cost Management + Billing is a free service that helps you understand your Azure bill, manage your account and subscriptions, monitor and control Azure spending, and optimize resource use. Which of the following is not a feature of Cost Management + Billing?

1. Budgeting
1. Alerting
2. Recommendations
3. Health monitoring

Correct Answer: 4

Explanation

Azure Cost Management + Billing features include:

- **Reporting:** Use historical data to generate reports and forecast future usage and expenditure.
- **Data enrichment:** Improve accountability by categorizing resources with tags that correspond to real-world business and organizational units.
- **Budgets:** Create and manage cost and usage budgets by monitoring resource demand trends, consumption rates, and cost patterns.
- **Alerting:** Get alerts based on your cost and usage budgets.
- **Recommendations:** Receive recommendations to eliminate idle resources and to optimize the Azure resources you provision.

17. Which one of the following actions is an example of transferring from IaaS to PaaS in order to cut charges?

1. Moving an SQL Database hosted on a virtual machine to Azure SQL Database
1. Moving a webapp to a virtual machine
2. Using Azure dedicated host instead of Virtual machines
3. Storing data in a Virtual Machine instead of Blob storage

Correct Answer: 1

Explanation

to reduce costs is to gradually move IaaS workloads to run on platform as a service (PaaS) service. While you can think of IaaS as direct access to compute infrastructure, PaaS provides ready-made development and deployment environments that are managed for you.

Ref:

- https://docs.microsoft.com/en-us/learn/modules/plan-manage-azure-costs/6-manage-minimize-total-cost

Software Assurance

18. If you've purchased licenses for Windows Server or SQL Server, you might be able to repurpose those licenses on VMs on Azure.

1. TRUE
1. FALSE

Correct Answer: 2

Explanation

If you've purchased licenses for Windows Server or SQL Server, and your licenses are covered by Software Assurance, you might be able to reuse those licenses on VMs on Azure and greatly reduce your incurred charges.

Ref:

* https://www.microsoft.com/en-us/licensing/licensing-programs/software-assurance-default?rtc=1&activetab=software-assurance-default-pivot%3aprimaryr3

Service-Level agreement (SLA)

19. What is a Service-level-agreement (SLA) ?

1. Agreement between Azure public cloud users on each ones role to ensure security.
   1. formal agreement between a service company and the customer.
2. Set of rules laid down by Azure regarding their services.
3. Rules that has been set by Azure to ensure sanity in their resources.

Correct Answer: 2

Explanation

A service-level agreement (SLA) is a formal agreement between a service company and the customer. For Azure, this agreement defines the performance standards that Microsoft commits to for you, the customer.

Ref:

- https://docs.microsoft.com/en-us/learn/modules/choose-azure-services-sla-lifecycle/2-what-are-service-level-agreements

20. Which of the following represents the formula to calculate monthly uptime percentage in Azure?

1. Maximum Available Minutes ? Downtime Minutes ? 100
   1. Maximum Available Minutes ? Minimum Available Minutes ? 100
2. (Maximum Available Minutes ? Downtime Minutes) Maximum Available Minutes ?
3. Downtime Minutes ? 60 ? 100

Correct Answer: 3

Explanation

"Monthly Uptime Percentage" for Virtual Machines in Availability Zones is calculated as Maximum Available Minutes less Downtime divided by Maximum Available Minutes in a billing month for a given Microsoft Azure subscription. Monthly Uptime Percentage is represented by the following formula:

Monthly Uptime % = (Maximum Available Minutes ? Downtime) / Maximum Available Minutes X 100

Ref:

- https://azure.microsoft.com/en-us/support/legal/sla/virtual-machines/v1_8/

21. What does downtime mean in regards to Azure SLA?

1. when the Azure region is down
1. Time duration that the service is unavailable.
2. Time taken to download data from Azure into local network
3. Time taken before a request sent to Azure is acknowledged

Correct Answer: 2

Explanation

Downtime refers to the time duration that the service is unavailable due to some circumstance that maybe affecting Azure datacenter where the resources you need are hosted leading to lack of services.

Ref:

https://azure.microsoft.com/en-us/support/legal/sla/

22. Having multiple backend Virtual Machines in Azure hosting a given app/website may offset the Composite SLA of that app/website. Which of the following actions may offset this reduction?

1. Increase the size of each virtual machine.
1. Cut the size of VMs by a half.
2. Use an Azure Load Balancer to increases the SLA for virtual machines.
3. Deploy extra instances of the same virtual machines across the different availability zones in the same Azure region.

Correct Answer: 4

Explanation

If one availability zone is affected, your virtual machine instance in the other availability zone should be unaffected and hence your services are still online. Increasing the VM size increases the charges and cutting the size may lead to slower services. Adding an Azure LB also will offset the composite SLA.

Ref:

- https://www.azure.cn/en-us/support/sla/virtual-machines/

23. You plan to deploy a critical line-of-business application to Azure that will run on an Azure virtual machine. You need to recommend a deployment solution for the application that must provide a guaranteed availability of 99.99 percent. What is the minimum number of virtual machines and the minimum number of availability zones you should recommend for the deployment?

1. Minimum number of virtual machines: 1
1. Minimum number of virtual machines: 2
2. Minimum number of virtual machines: 3
3. Minimum number of availability zones: 1

4. Minimum number of availability zones: 2
5. Minimum number of availability zones: 3

Correct Answer: 2,5

Explanation

For all Virtual Machines that have two or more instances deployed across two or more Availability Zones in the same Azure region, will guarantee you will have Virtual Machine Connectivity to at least one instance at least 99.99% of the time. There is no additional cost for virtual machines deployed in an Availability Zone. 99.99% VM uptime SLA is offered when two or more VMs are deployed across two or more Availability Zones within an Azure region.

Ref:

- https://docs.microsoft.com/en-us/azure/availability-zones/az-overview & https://azure.microsoft.com/en-us/support/legal/sla/virtual-machines/v1_9/

24. What does application availability refer to according to Microsoft Azure Services?

1. Application support for availability zones in azure
1. Service Level agreement (SLA) of associated resources
2. Overall time that the system is up and running
3. Inclusion of the application into availability set on Azure

Correct Answer: 3

Explanation

Availability refers to the overall time that the is working as it is expected with no downtime. Availability time lets you decide if Azure meets the service Level Agreement regarding the uptime of their services and the effects downtime could have on application accessibility.

Ref:

- https://docs.microsoft.com/en-us/azure/azure-monitor/app/monitor-web-app-availability

25. All paying Azure customers can claim a credit if their monthly uptime percentage is below the guaranteed amount in the Service Level Agreement (SLA).

1. TRUE
1. FALSE

Correct Answer: 1

Explanation

You can claim credit if the availability falls below the SLA. The amount of credit depends on the availability. For example: You can claim 25% credit if the availability is less than 99.9%, 50% credit for less than 99% and 100% for less than 95% availability on Azure.

Ref:

- https://www.azure.cn/en-us/support/sla/virtual-machines/

26. You have deployed some Azure resources and they become unavailable for an extended period due to a service outage. Microsoft will?

1. refund your bank account.
1. migrate the resource to another subscription
2. credit your account
3. send you a coupon code that you can redeem for Azure credits

Correct Answer: 3

Explanation

If Azure do not achieve and maintain the Service Levels for each Service as described in this SLA, then you may be eligible for a credit towards a portion of your monthly service fees. We will not modify the terms of your SLA during the initial term of your subscription; however, if you renew your subscription, the version of this SLA that is current at the time of renewal will apply throughout your renewal term. We will provide at least 90 days' notice for adverse material changes to this SLA.

Ref:

- https://azure.microsoft.com/en-in/support/legal/sla/app-service/v1_4

Azure Status

27. Where do you check when you suspect azure services outage in a certain region?
Multiple-choice

1. Azure Monitor
1. Azure Status
2. Azure Health services
3. Azure Advisor

Correct Answer: 2

Explanation

Azure status provides a global view of the health of Azure services and regions. If you suspect there's an outage, this is often a good place to start your investigation. From the Azure status page, you can also access Azure Service Health. This provides a personalized view of the health of the Azure services and regions that you're using, directly from the Azure portal.

Ref:

- https://status.azure.com/status

Composite SLA

28. Your company hosts an app on Azure that requires 2 VMs, one SQL database and one Load balancer. The company SLA for each of those Azure features is 99.9% uptime. What is the composite SLA of the hosted app?

1. 99.95%
1. 99.90%
2. 99.78%
3. 99.99%

Correct Answer: 3

Explanation

You get SLA of composite SLA by multiplying all the SLAs of the resources being utilized by the application. So, the composite SLA of the app is 99.9% ? 99.9% ? 99.9% ? 99.9%.

Ref:

- https://docs.microsoft.com/en-us/learn/modules/choose-azure-services-sla-lifecycle/4-design-application-meet-sla

•

Azure Service lifecycle

29. What is Service life cycle in Azure?

1. defines how cloud services are deployed and terminated.
1. defines how every Azure service is released for public use.
2. defines the route followed to purchase an Azure resource.
3. defines how Azure SLA is made.

Correct Answer: 2

Explanation

Service life cycle explains how a product is moved all the way from development phase to when it is Available to public for use.

Ref:

- https://docs.microsoft.com/en-us/learn/modules/choose-azure-services-sla-lifecycle/5-access-preview-services

30. After a new Azure service is validated and tested, it's released to all customers as a production-ready service phase is called?

1. Public review
1. General Availability
2. Private review
3. DMarketplace

Correct Answer: 2

Explanation

General Availability (GA) is the release of a product to the general public. When a product reaches GA, it becomes available through the company?s general sales channel ? as opposed to a limited release, or beta version, used primarily for testing and user feedback purposes.

Ref:

- https://docs.microsoft.com/en-us/learn/modules/choose-azure-services-sla-lifecycle/5-access-preview-services

31. Your company hosts an app on Azure. What approach might your company take in adding the augmented reality (AR) preview service to its architecture?

1. The app is already in production. The company shouldn't look into the AR service until the service reaches general availability (GA).
1. The app is mainly for use by employees. The company can integrate the AR service now because potential downtime or failures aren't an important factor.
2. The development team can create a prototype version of the app that includes the AR service that it tests out with select employees.

Correct Answer: 3

Explanation

After the AR service reaches general availability (GA), the team can roll it out to production.

32. What does it mean if a service is in General Availability (GA) mode?

1. You have to apply to get selected in order to use that service
1. Anyone can use the service but it must not be for production use
2. The service is generally available for use, and Microsoft will provide support for it
3. Anyone can use the service for any reason

Correct Answer: 4

Explanation

When an Azure service is listed under General Availability category, it means that the service is open to be used by anyone. It is fully supported and can be used for production purposes by a company.

Ref:

- https://azure.microsoft.com/en-au/updates/announcing-the-general-availability-of-azure-lab-services/

Azure service limits

33. You attempt to create several managed Microsoft SQL Server instances in an Azure environment and receive a message that you must increase your Azure subscription limits.
What should you do to increase the limits?

1. A Create a service health alert
1. Upgrade your support plan
2. Modify an Azure policy
3. Create a new support request

Correct Answer: 4

Explanation

Create a new support request> The limit for Azure resources can be raised above the default limit but not above the maximum limit. If you want to raise the limit or quota above the default limit, open an online customer support request at no charge

Ref:

- https://docs.microsoft.com/en-us/azure/azure-subscription-service-limits

Spot VMS

34. Which of the following options is the main advantage of using Spot Virtual Machines in Azure?

1. Spot VMs have SLA of 99.999% so downtime is very rare
1. When using Spot VMs you only pay VM and not other resources being utilized by the VM
2. Spot VMs allows you to take advantage of unused capacity at a significant cost savings
3. Spot VMs has low latency compared to other VMs hence faster

Correct Answer: 3

Explanation

Using Spot VMs allows you to take advantage of our unused capacity at a significant cost savings. At any point in time when Azure needs the capacity back, the Azure infrastructure will evict Spot VMs. Therefore, Spot VMs are great for workloads that can handle interruptions like batch processing jobs, dev/test environments, large compute workloads, and more.

Ref:

- https://docs.microsoft.com/en-us/azure/virtual-machines/spot-portal

35. Which is the main disadvantage of using Azure Spot Virtual Machine for your workload?

1. You have to pay almost double the price for a Spot VM compared to normal VM
1. There is no SLA for Spot VMs
2. Azure can delete Spot VMs with your data without a warning
3. Spot VMs has high latency and hence a bit slow

Explanation

When deploying Spot VMs, Azure will allocate the VMs if there is capacity available, but there is no SLA for these VMs. A Spot VM offers no high availability guarantees. At any point in time when Azure needs the capacity back, the Azure infrastructure will evict Spot VMs with 30 second?s notice.

Ref:

- https://docs.microsoft.com/en-us/azure/virtual-machines/spot-vms

36. Spot Virtual Machines can be deployed in any region/block globally expect which one?

1. Azure Germany
1. Azure US Governance
2. Azure South Africa
3. Azure China 21Vianet

Correct Answer: 4

Explanation

Spot VMs can be deployed to any region, except Microsoft Azure China 21Vianet. Microsoft Azure in China is a public cloud platform that is operated and sold independently by 21Vianet in China mainland. 21vianet do not offer Spot VM instances and hence the service is unavailable in china but you can always use any other public region worldwide to use Spot VMs.

Ref:

- https://docs.microsoft.com/en-us/azure/virtual-machines/spot-vms

37. Which of the following actions are you required to take first before you can change the Maximum price of a Spot VM?

1. Deallocate the Spot VM
1. Get a support ticket
2. Delete the VM.
3. You cannot change the max price in a Spot VM

Correct Answer: 1

Explanation

Before you can change the max price, you need to deallocate/stop the VM. Then you can change the max price in the portal, from the Configuration section for the VM. VMs can be evicted based on capacity or the max price you set. When creating a Spot VM, you can set the eviction policy to Deallocate (default) or Delete.

Ref:

- https://docs.microsoft.com/en-us/azure/virtual-machines/spot-vms

38. What happens in a Spot VM scenario when the current price exceeds the maximum price you set?

1. Nothing happens you continue being charged
1. The Spot VM changes to standard VM
2. The VM is evicted
3. The VM is restarted

Correct Answer: 3

Explanation

When Price for the Spot VM has gone up and is now greater than the set max price, The VM gets evicted. You get a 30s notification before actual eviction. When creating a Spot VM, you can set the eviction policy to Deallocate (default) or Delete.

39. Which of the following scenarios would be well suited for spot VMs instances?

1. A database for a business-critical financial application.
1. Virtual desktops for employees.
2. A system that enables patients to access health records.
3. A system that processes batches of data that is sent from partners.

Correct Answer: 4

Explanation

Using Spot VMs allows you to take advantage of our unused capacity at a significant cost savings. Therefore, Spot VMs are great for workloads that can handle interruptions like batch processing jobs, dev/test environments, large compute workloads, and more.

Ref:

- https://docs.microsoft.com/en-us/azure/virtual-machines/spot-portal

VM Scale sets

40. Azure virtual machine scale sets let you create and manage a group of load balanced VMs. Scale sets provide high availability to your applications, and allow you to centrally manage, configure, and update a large number of VMs. Is it possible to have an Azure Scale set made of both Spot VMs and Standard VMs?

1. TRUE
1. FALSE

Correct Answer: 2

Explanation

Scale sets only support one priority type of Azure VMs in this case either Standard VMs or Spot VMs. If you have both standard and spot VMs you will be forced to create different scale sets for each of the type.

Ref:

- https://docs.microsoft.com/en-us/azure/virtual-machine-scale-sets/use-spot

Resrved Instancs

41. On Azure reserved instances, reservation discount only applies to resources associated with subscriptions purchased through the following EXCEPT which one?

1. Enterprise
1. Microsoft Special Clients
2. Cloud Solution Provider (CSP)
3. Microsoft Customer Agreement

Correct Answer: 2

Explanation

A reservation discount only applies to resources associated with subscriptions purchased through Enterprise, Cloud Solution Provider (CSP), Microsoft Customer Agreement, and individual plans with pay-as-you-go rates.

Ref:

- https://docs.microsoft.com/en-us/learn/modules/save-money-with-azure-reserved-instances/3-buy-reservation

42. What reservation scope should be used to share benefits across subscriptions?

1. Resource group scope
1. Enrolment Account scope
2. Shared scope
3. Pay-as-you-go scope

Correct Answer: 3

Explanation

The shared scope applies the reservation discount to matching resources of subscriptions that are in the billing context:

*For Enterprise Agreement customers, the billing context is the enrolment.

*For Microsoft Customer Agreement customers, the billing scope is the billing profile.

*For individual subscriptions with pay-as-you-go rates, the billing scope is all eligible subscriptions created by the account administrator.

Ref:

- https://docs.microsoft.com/en-us/learn/modules/save-money-with-azure-reserved-instances/3-buy-reservation

43. Which Azure customer types are supported by Azure reservations?

1. Enterprise Agreement, Web-direct, CSP, and Microsoft Customer Agreement
1. MPN credit subscriptions, Free Trial, and MSDN credit subscriptions
2. BizSpark, Azure in Open, and the Microsoft Azure for Students Starter Offer

Correct Answer: 1

Explanation

All the customer types shown are supported with Azure reservations except the Free trial and Microsoft Azure Students Starter offer which cannot purchase a reservation in Azure.

Ref:

- https://docs.microsoft.com/en-us/learn/modules/save-money-with-azure-reserved-instances/3-buy-reservation

44. What is one way of optimizing your reservation purchase?

1. Exchange unused quantity for a different reservation
1. Assign new user?s permissions on the reservation
2. Enable instance region flexibility
3. Terminate reservations when underutilized

Reservations can be optimized by exchanging an unused quantity for a different reservation. Purchasing more capacity than your historical usage results in an underutilized reservation. You should avoid underutilization whenever possible. Unused reserved capacity doesn't carry over from one hour to next. Usage exceeding the reserved quantity is charged using more expensive pay-as-you-go rates.

Ref:

- https://docs.microsoft.com/en-us/azure/cost-management-billing/reservations/determine-reservation-purchase

45. What report type is used to create charge back report?

1. Actual Cost report
1. RI Savings report
2. Amortized Cost report
3. Total Cost report

Correct Answer: 3

Explanation

The amortized report in Cost Management shows costs over the course of your reservation period. Amortized Cost dataset is similar to the Actual Cost dataset except that - the EffectivePrice for the usage that gets reservation discount is the prorated cost of the reservation (instead of being zero). This helps you know the monetary value of reservation consumption by a subscription, resource group or a resource, and can help you charge back for the reservation utilization internally.

Ref:

- https://docs.microsoft.com/en-us/azure/cost-management-billing/reservations/understand-reserved-instance-usage-ea

46. Describe Azure reservation

1. Having resources in Azure reserved for you till you need them
1. Committing to one-year or three-year plans for multiple products on Azure for discounted price.
2. Having dedicated resources in Azure for low latency

Correct Answer: 2

Explanation

Azure Reservations help you save money by committing to one-year or three-year plans for multiple products. Committing allows you to get a discount on the resources you use. Reservations can significantly reduce your resource costs by up to 72% from pay-as-you-go prices. Reservations provide a billing discount and don't affect the runtime state of your resources. After you purchase a reservation, the discount automatically applies to matching resources.

Ref:

- https://docs.microsoft.com/en-us/azure/cost-management-billing/reservations/save-compute-costs-reservations

47. How are Azure reservations applied on periodic terms?

1. Yearly
1. 3 years
2. Hourly
3. Monthly

Correct Answer: 3

Explanation

All reservations, except Azure Databricks, are applied on an hourly basis. Consider reservation purchases based on your consistent base usage. You can determine which reservation to purchase by analyzing your usage data or by using reservation recommendations.

Ref:

- https://docs.microsoft.com/en-us/azure/cost-management-billing/reservations/save-compute-costs-reservations

48. Which of the following scenarios would benefit from the use of reserved instances?

1. You have a workload that needs a VPN connection between Azure and an on-premises datacenter.
1. You have a website that needs the flexibility to scale from hundreds to millions of users at any point in time.
2. You have an enterprise resource planning (ERP) system with consistent resource utilization.
3. You have a small administrative task that uses PowerShell that you want to run automatically.

Correct Answer: 3

Explanation

Azure Reservations help you save money by committing to one-year or three-year plans for multiple products. Committing allows you to get a discount on the resources you use. Reservations can significantly reduce your resource costs by up to 72% from pay-as-you-go prices. Reservations provide a billing discount and don't affect the runtime state of your resources. After you purchase a reservation, the discount automatically applies to matching resources.

Ref:

- https://docs.microsoft.com/en-us/azure/cost-management-billing/reservations/save-compute-costs-reservation

Azure Advisor

49. Which of the following tools found in the Azure portal can be used to help determine what to buy for a reservation purchase?

1. The last page of your monthly invoice
   1. Azure Advisor
2. Cost Insights in the Azure portal
3. Azure Pricing calculator

Correct Answer: 2

Explanation

Azure Advisor shows reservation purchase recommendations that will greatly save your charges in Azure including reservation instances that maybe available for you.

Ref:

- https://azure.microsoft.com/en-us/blog/new-recommendations-in-azure-advisor

Account Permissions

50. Which of the following roles is used to manage costs in your company's billing hierarchy?

1. Global admin agent
1. Owner
2. Billing profile admin
3. Account holder

Correct Answer: 1

Explanation

The global admin agent role can manage costs for the company. The admin agent role can also manage costs, View, create, and manage billing, invoices, and recon files.

Ref:

- https://docs.microsoft.com/en-us/partner-center/permissions-overview

Partner Center

51. What dimension can you use in cost analysis to determine whether a resource charge has received partner earned credit?

1. PartnerCredit
1. PartnerEarnedCreditApplied
2. IsPartnerCreditApplied

Correct Answer: 2

Explanation

in cost analysis, the PartnerEarnedCreditApplied dimension is shown as True when the credit is applicable. It's shown as False when it isn't applicable. Partner earned credit for managed services (PEC) recognizes and rewards partners that own the 24x7 IT operational control and management of parts of, or the entire, Azure environment of their customers.

Ref:

- https://docs.microsoft.com/en-us/partner-center/partner-earned-credit-explanation

Azure Pricing Calculator

52. Which of the following tools can you use to estimate costs for a new application you are deploying on Azure?

1. Azure Resource Manager
1. Azure Policy
2. Azure Cost Management
3. Azure Pricing Calculator

Correct Answer: 4

Explanation

Azure Pricing Calculator can be used to estimate costs for services used for a new application on Azure to help plan for cloud deployment by estimating resources you will need.

Ref:

- https://azure.microsoft.com/en-us/pricing/calculator/

53. Which of the following would be an example of a cost anomaly that you should investigate further?

1. 1% increase in compute costs from the previous month.
1. A decrease in compute costs after the decommission of a website.
2. A 5% increase in storage costs after the migration of a large database.
3. A 25% increase in ExpressRoute circuit utilization from the previous month.

Correct Answer: 4

Explanation

25% is a large spike in utilization and would merit further investigation especially if you have not increased your resources that utilize the ExpressRoute circuit by a similar percent or more.

Ref:

- https://azure.microsoft.com/en-us/pricing/details/cognitive-services/anomaly-detector/

Elastic Pools

54. Which of the following databases would be well suited for elastic pools?

1. An ERP database that has consistent usage around the clock.
1. Customer databases that have usage during the same period of time.
2. Customer databases that are spread across time zones and have periods of intermittent usage.

Correct Answer: 1

Explanation

Because these databases are used intermittently, their resources could be shared, making them good candidates for elastic pools.

PART 2

Describe Cloud Concepts

Pricing

1. Cloud computing is the delivery of computing services over the internet by using a pay-as-you-go pricing model. You typically pay only for the cloud services you use, which helps you?

1. Lower your operating costs
1. Run your infrastructure more efficiently
2. Arrange your servers more efficiently
3. Ensure that you are directly responsible for server?s security
4. Scale as your business needs change

Correct Answer: 1,2,5

Explanation

Cloud computing is a way to rent compute power and storage from someone else's datacenter. You can treat cloud resources like you would your resources in your own datacenter. When you're done using them, you give them back. You're billed only for what you use.> Cloud computing is a way to rent compute power and storage from someone else's datacenter. You can treat cloud resources like you would your resources in your own datacenter. When you're done using them, you give them back. You're billed only for what you use.

Instead of maintaining CPUs and storage in your datacenter, you rent them for the time that you need them. The cloud provider takes care of maintaining the underlying infrastructure for you. The cloud enables you to quickly solve your toughest business challenges and bring cutting-edge solutions to your users.Reference:

- https://docs.microsoft.com/en-us/learn/modules/intro-to-azure-fundamentals/what-is-cloud-computing

2. Azure Cloud service operate on a consumption-based model or popularly known as Pay-As-You-Go model, which means that end users only pay for whatever they use. Which of the following 2 choices are the main benefits of this payment model?

1. No upfront costs.
1. No need for payment until you have exhausted all the services.
2. You are billed once per annum
3. No need to purchase and manage costly infrastructure that users might not use to its fullest.
4. The ability to pay for additional resources when they are not needed

Correct Answer: 1,4

Explanation

pay-as-you-go model means usage is metered and you pay only for what you consume. The fundamental economics of cloud computing are based around the premise that customers will pay for how long a server is used, or how much bandwidth data is being consumed

Ref:

- https://docs.microsoft.com/en-us/azure/architecture/framework/cost/design-price

Cloud Models

3. There are several benefits that a cloud environment has over a physical environment server. Which of the following is/are the advantages of having cloud compared to having a physical local environment?

1. High network latency
1. High elasticity
2. More capital expenditure
3. Disaster recovery
4. Dynamic scalability

Correct Answer: 2,4,5

Explanation

High availability: Depending on the service-level agreement that you choose, your cloud-based applications can provide a continuous user experience with no apparent downtime even when things go wrong.

Scalability: Applications in the cloud can be scaled in two ways:

- **Vertically:** Computing capacity can be increased by adding RAM or CPUs to a virtual machine.
- **Horizontally:** Computing capacity can be increased by adding instances of a resource, such as adding more virtual machines to your configuration.

Disaster recovery: By taking advantage of cloud-based backup services, data replication, and geo-distribution, you can deploy your applications with the confidence that comes from knowing that your data is safe in the event that disaster should occur.

Ref:

- https://docs.microsoft.com/en-us/learn/modules/intro-to-azure-fundamentals/what-is-cloud-computing

4. Where do you go within the Azure Portal to find all of the third-party virtual machine VHDs and other offers?

1. Azure mobile app
1. creating a VM
2. Choose an image when
3. Azure Marketplace
4. Microsoft Bing

Correct Answer: 3

Explanation

Azure Marketplace contains thousands of services you can rent within the cloud. It helps connect users with Microsoft partners, independent software vendors, and start-ups that are offering their solutions and services, which are optimized to run on Azure. Azure Marketplace customers can find, try, purchase, and provision applications and services from hundreds of leading service providers. All solutions and services are certified to run on Azure.

Ref:

- https://docs.microsoft.com/en-us/learn/modules/intro-to-azure-fundamentals/what-is-microsoft-azure

Cloud Models

5. If your company Computing resources are physically located at your organization's on-site datacenter hosted by a third-party service provider, which cloud deployment model does your company employ?

1. Hybrid Cloud
1. Public Cloud
2. Private Cloud
3. Public-Private Cloud

Correct Answer: 3

Explanation

private cloud is a single-tenant environment, meaning the organization using it (the tenant) does not share resources with other users. Those resources can be hosted and managed in a variety of ways. The private cloud might be based on resources and infrastructure already present in an organization's on-premises data center or on new, separate infrastructure, which is provided by a third-party organization.

Ref:

- https://azure.microsoft.com/en-us/overview/what-is-a-private-cloud/

6. Azure offers public cloud services model which is different from physical/private public cloud model where owners have their own server network. Which of the below listed operations are attributes of public cloud model?

1. Have metred pricing
1. Have dedicated hardware

2. Have unsecured network connection
3. Have Limited Storage
4. Have Self-service Management

Correct Answer: 4,5

Explanation

To power your services and deliver innovative and novel user experiences more quickly, the cloud provides on-demand access to:

- A nearly limitless pool of raw compute, storage, and networking components.
- Speech recognition and other cognitive services that help make your application stand out from the crowd.

Ref:

- https://docs.microsoft.com/en-us/learn/modules/intro-to-azurefundamentals/what-is-cloud-computing

7. You plan to migrate several servers from an on-premises network to Azure.What is an advantage of using a public cloud service for the servers over an on-premises network?

1. The public cloud is owned by the public, NOT a private corporation
1. The public cloud is a crowd-sourcing solution that provides corporations with the ability to enhance the cloud
2. All public cloud resources can be freely accessed by every member of the public
3. The public cloud is a shared entity whereby multiple corporations each use a portion of the resources in the cloud

Correct Answer: 4

Explanation

The public cloud is a shared entity whereby multiple corporations each use a portion of the resources in the cloud. The hardware resources (servers, infrastructure etc.) are managed by the cloud provider. Multiple companies create resources such as virtual machines and virtual networks on the hardware resources.

- https://azure.microsoft.com/en-us/overview/what-is-cloud-computing/

8. Can you identify from below a Setup that represents a hybrid cloud model

1. An Azure Web Application Program interface that connects to an on-premises SQL Server database at an on-premises private datacenter
   1. An Azure Web job that makes calls to the Azure Representational state Transfer (REST) application program interface
2. An Azure web application that connects to an azure SQL Database
3. An Azure function crawls the web for trending news

Correct Answer: 1

Explanation

Hybrid cloud computing refers to a computing environment that combines public cloud and on-premises infrastructure, including private cloud, by allowing data and applications to be shared between them. ... It's evolving to include multicloud environments and edge infrastructure.

- https://azure.microsoft.com/en-us/solutions/hybrid-cloud-app/#:~:text=Hybrid%20cloud%20computing%20refers%20to,to%20be%20shared%20between%20them.&text=It's%20evolving%20to%20include%20multicloud%20environments%20and%20edge%20infrastructure.

9. You have been contracted by a company that a local network with over 100 servers to recommend a solution to them that will provide additional resources to their customers at a minimum capital and operation expenditure costs. Which of the following solutions could you recommend?

1. a complete migration to the public cloud
1. an additional data center
2. a private cloud
3. a hybrid cloud

Correct Answer: 4

Explanation

With a hybrid cloud, you can continue to use the on-premises servers while adding new servers in the public cloud (Azure for example). Adding new servers in Azure minimizes the capital expenditure costs as you are not paying for new servers as you would if you deployed new server on-premises.

Ref:

- https://azure.microsoft.com/en-us/overview/what-are-private-public-hybrid-clouds/

Expenditure Models

10. What is the one name given to Azure?s Pay-As-You-Go rate model of service charging?

1. Operational model
1. Capital model
2. Consumption-based model
3. Fixed-Price model

Correct Answer: 3

Explanation

On Consumption-based price model, you get charged for only the services that your azure resources have directly used or what you have used. This model is also known as the Pay-As-You-Go.

Ref:

- https://docs.microsoft.com/en-us/azure/architecture/framework/cost/design-price

Resource groups

11. When you need to delegate permissions to several Azure virtual machines simultaneously, you must deploy the Azure virtual machines to?

1. the same Azure region.
1. by using the same Azure Resource Manager template.
2. to the same resource group.
3. to the same availability zone

Correct Answer: 3

Explanation

A resource group is a logical container for Azure resources. Resource groups make the management of Azure resources easier. With a resource group, you can allow a user to manage all resources in the resource group, such as virtual machines, websites, and subnets. The permissions you apply to the resource group apply to all resources contained in the resource group.

Ref:

- https://docs.microsoft.com/en-us/azure/role-based-access-control/role-assignments-portal

12. A container that holds related resources for an Azure solution usually based under subscription on Azure is called?

1. A resource
1. A management group
2. A Resource group
3. Marketplace

Correct Answer: 3

Explanation

The resource group includes resources that you want to manage as a group. You decide which resources belong in a resource group based on what makes the most sense for your organization. Resource is manageable item that's available through Azure. Virtual machines (VMs), storage accounts, web apps, databases, and virtual networks are examples of resources.

Ref:

- https://docs.microsoft.com/en-us/learn/modules/azure-architecture-fundamentals/resources-resource-manager

13. Which of the following features doesn't apply to resource groups?

1. Resources can only be in one resource group
1. Role-Based Access Control can be applied to resource groups
2. Resource groups can be nested
3. Resource groups can?t be in multiple subscriptions

Correct Answer: 3

Explanation

Resource groups cannot be Nested (a Resource group that contains other Resource groups), and consequently, when assigning user permissions to a resource group, it is simpler to create a single resource group and include all the needed resource in that group.

REF:

- https://docs.microsoft.com/en-us/azure/azure-resource-manager/templates/deploy-to-resource-group?tabs=azure-cli

Network Services

14. Which of following Azure Services is/are NOT offered by Azure under the Networking category?

1. A. Azure Load Balancer
1. Azure Virtual Network
2. Azure Virtual Machine
3. Azure Fabric Services
4. Azure Application Gateway

Correct Answer: 3,4

Explanation

Azure Network services categories contains Azure VN, Azure App Gateway, Azure Firewall, Azure Load balancer, Azure DDoS protection, Network watcher, Azure CDN, Azure Expressroute and Azure Traffic manager.

Azure VMs and Fabric services fall under Azure Compute Services.

Ref:

- https://docs.microsoft.com/en-us/learn/modules/intro-to-azure-fundamentals/tour-of-azure-services

Storage Services

15. Which Azure Storage is perfect for storing large objects such as Virtual Hard disks(VHDs), Videos, large compressed files and bitmap images?

1. Azure Queue Storage
1. Azure File storage
2. Azure Blob Storage
3. Azure Table Storage

Correct Answer: 3

Explanation

Blob storage: Storage service for very large objects, such as video files or bitmaps.Azure File storage: File shares that can be accessed and managed like a file server.

Azure Queue storage: A data store for queuing and reliably delivering messages between applications.

Azure Table Azure storage: A NoSQL store that hosts unstructured data independent of any schema.

Ref:

- https://docs.microsoft.com/en-us/azure/storage/common/storage-introduction

16. Your company has a group of developers working on developing a certain application over the Azure cloud. The developers have to share some files that will be accessed by every Vm connected to a certain network. Which type of Azure storage will be the best fit for this kind of work?

1. Azure Queue Storage

1. Azure File storage
2. Azure Blob Storage
3. Azure Table Storage

Correct Answer: 2

Explanation

Azure Files enables you to set up highly available network file shares that can be accessed by using the standard Server Message Block (SMB) protocol. That means that multiple VMs can share the same files with both read and write access. You can also read the files using the REST interface or the storage client libraries.

One thing that distinguishes Azure Files from files on a corporate file share is that you can access the files from anywhere in the world using a URL that points to the file and includes a shared access signature (SAS) token. You can generate SAS tokens; they allow specific access to a private asset for a specific amount of time.

Ref:

- https://docs.microsoft.com/en-us/azure/storage/files/storage-files-introduction

17. Which of the following is optimized for storing massive amounts of unstructured data, such as videos and images?

1. Blobs
1. Files
2. Queues
3. VHDs

Correct Answer: 1

Explanation

Azure Blob storage is Microsoft?s object storage solution for the cloud. Blob storage is optimized for storing massive amounts of unstructured data, such as text or binary data.

Ref:

- https://azure.microsoft.com/en-us/services/storage/blobs/

Big Data

18. Big Data refers to very large volumes of data coming from maybe an imaging app like Instagram ,weather systems or communication systems that generate Terabytes of data in a short period. Which of the following Big Data service offered by Azure takes advantage of massively parallel processing to run complex queries quickly across petabytes of data?

1. Azure Databricks
1. Azure HDInsight
2. Azure Datalake
3. Azure Synapse Analytics

Correct Answer: 4

Explanation

Azure Synapse Analytics is used to run analytics at a massive scale by using a cloud-based enterprise data warehouse that takes advantage of massively parallel processing to run complex queries quickly across petabytes of data.

Ref:

- https://azure.microsoft.com/en-us/solutions/big-data/

Infrastracture as a service

19. Which of the following services Provided by Azure Cloud fall under the Infrastructure as a Service (Iaas) category?

1. Microsoft Office 365
1. Azure Kubernetes Services
2. Azure Virtual Machine
3. Azure SQL Database

Correct Answer: 3

Explanation

Azure Virtual Machine. > Infrastructure as a service (IaaS) is an instant computing infrastructure, provisioned and managed over the internet. IaaS quickly scales up and down with demand, letting you pay only for what you use. It helps you avoid the expense and complexity of buying and managing your own physical servers and other datacentre infrastructure. Each resource is offered as a separate service component, and you only need to rent a particular one for as long as you need it. Azure, manages the infrastructure, while you purchase, install, configure, and manage your own software?operating systems, middleware, and applications and hence Azure Virtual Machines are under this category since you have to install the Operating System on them on your own.

Ref:

- https://azure.microsoft.com/en-us/overview/what-is-iaas/

Infrastructure Models

20. Which of the following is the correct match for the Microsoft provided services and the cloud service model the fall under?
i. Office 365
ii. Azure App services
iii. Azure Virtual Machines

1. Iaas ? Azure App services, PaaS- Office365, SaaS- Azure VMs
1. IaaS-Azure VMs, PaaS-Azure App services, SaaS-Office365
2. IaaS- Office365, PaaS- Azure VMs, SaaS- Azure App Services
3. IaaS- Azure VMs, PaaS- Office365, SaaS- Azure App services

Correct Answer: 2

Explanation

Iaas: This cloud model is the closest to managing physical servers. A cloud provider keeps the hardware up to date, but operating system maintenance and network configuration is left to the cloud tenant. For example, Azure virtual machines.

PaaS: This cloud service model is a managed hosting environment. The cloud provider manages the virtual machines and networking resources, and the cloud tenant deploys their applications into the managed hosting environment. For example, Azure App Services.

SaaS: In this cloud service model, the cloud provider manages all aspects of the application environment, such as virtual machines, networking resources, data storage, and applications. The cloud tenant only needs to provide their data to the application managed by the cloud provider. For example, Office 365.

Databases

21. Which of the following Azure provided Database options does NOT support SQL options?

1. Azure for MariaDB
1. Azure Cosmos DB
2. Azure SQL Database
3. Azure for PostgreSQL

Correct Answer: 2

Explanation

Azure Cosmos DB is a fully managed NoSQL database for modern app development. Single-digit millisecond response times, and automatic and instant scalability, guarantee speed at any scale. Business continuity is assured with SLA-backed availability and enterprise-grade security.

Ref:

- https://docs.microsoft.com/en-us/azure/cosmos-db/introduction

Machine Learning

22. Which service could your company use to build, test, and deploy predictive analytics solutions?

1. Azure Logic Apps
1. Azure Machine Learning studio
2. Azure HDInsight
3. Azure Artificial Intelligence

Correct Answer: 2

Explanation

Azure Machine learning studio is a Collaborative visual workspace where you can build, test, and deploy machine learning solutions by using prebuilt machine learning algorithms and data-handling modules.

Ref:

- https://docs.microsoft.com/en-us/azure/machine-learning/overview-what-is-machine-learning-studio

23. You have a Robot vacuum cleaner in your home that helps you in keeping the house clean. When the robot vacuums the room, which of the following services offered in azure that can help the robot decide if the room is clean enough or still dirty?

1. Azure Knowledge mapping
1. Azure Logic Apps service
2. Azure Machine Learning
3. Azure cognitive service.

Correct Answer: 3

Explanation

Machine learning is a data science technique that allows computers to use existing data to forecast future behaviours, outcomes, and trends. Using machine learning, computers learn without being explicitly programmed. Forecasts or predictions from machine learning can make apps and devices smarter.

Ref:

- https://docs.microsoft.com/en-us/azure/machine-learning/overview-what-is-machine-learning-studio

Azure Resource Manager

24. Azure Resource Manager templates use which format?

1. HTML
1. JSON
2. XML
3. XHTML

Correct Answer: 2

Explanation

Resource Manager templates are JSON files that define the resources you need to deploy for your solution. You can use a template to easily re-create multiple versions of your infrastructure, such as staging and production.

Ref:

- https://docs.microsoft.com/en-us/azure/templates/

25. Which azure resource enables thread level authorization such that When a user sends a request from any of the Azure tools, APIs, or SDKs, the resource receives the request. It authenticates and authorizes the request. It then sends the request to the Azure service, which takes the requested action.

1. Azure Resource Group
1. Azure Management Group
2. Azure Resources manager
3. Azure Marketplace

Correct Answer: 3

Explanation

Azure Resource Manager is the deployment and management service for Azure. It provides a management layer that enables you to create, update, and delete resources in your Azure account. You use management features like access control, locks, and tags to secure and organize your resources after deployment.When a user sends a request from any of the Azure tools, APIs, or SDKs, Resource Manager receives the request. It authenticates and authorizes the request. Resource Manager sends the request to the Azure service, which takes the requested action. Because all requests are handled through the same API, you see consistent results and capabilities in all the different tools.

Ref:

- https://docs.microsoft.com/en-us/learn/modules/azure-architecture-fundamentals/resources-resource-manager

Azure Accounts

26. The Azure free account is an excellent way for new users to get started and explore. Which of following listed things does NOT come with the Azure Free account?

1. Free access to popular Azure products for 12 months.
1. Free storage account with 5GB capacity
2. $200 credit to spend for the first 30 days.
3. Access to more than 25 products that are always free.

Correct Answer: 2

Explanation

The Azure free account includes access to a number of Azure products that are free for 12 months, $200 credit to spend for the first 30 days of sign up, and access to more than 25 products that are always free.

Ref:

- https://azure.microsoft.com/en-us/free/free-account-faq/

Serverless computing

27. Which of the following statement BEST describes Serverless computing as a service provided by Microsoft Azure?

1. service that enables developers to develop their webapps without computers
1. A service that does not depend on servers to complete computations
2. A service that enables developers to build applications faster by eliminating the need for them to manage infrastructure
3. A service that enables developers to come app with applications without coding

Correct Answer: 4

Explanation

understanding the definition of serverless computing, it?s important to note that servers are still running the code. The serverless name comes from the fact that the tasks associated with infrastructure provisioning and management are invisible to the developer. This approach enables developers to increase their focus on the business logic and deliver more value to the core of the business. Serverless computing helps teams increase their productivity and bring products to market faster, and it allows organizations to better optimize resources and stay focused on innovation.

Ref:

- https://azure.microsoft.com/en-us/overview/serverless-computing/

Elasticity

28. Your company hosts a salary payment processing App that has very low usage on the first three weeks of the month and very high usage on the last 1 week of the month. Which benefit of Azure Cloud Services supports cost management for this type of usage pattern?

1. high availability
1. high latency
2. elasticity
3. load balancing

Correct Answer: 3

Explanation

Elastic computing is the ability to quickly expand or decrease computer processing, memory, and storage resources to meet changing demands without worrying about capacity planning and engineering for peak usage. Typically controlled by system monitoring tools, elastic computing matches the amount of resources allocated to the amount of resources actually needed without disrupting operations. With cloud elasticity, a company avoids paying for unused capacity or idle resources and doesn't have to worry about investing in the purchase or maintenance of additional resources and equipment.

Ref:

- https://azure.microsoft.com/en-us/overview/what-is-elastic-computing/

Subscriptions

29. Your company plans to extend their network to public cloud services specifically Microsoft Azure. As the Network administrator, you have been tasked with the job of exploring all Azure services and coming up with the best plan and cost estimation for the planned extension. What is the first thing you should create after getting an Azure account?

1. A resource Group
1. Your Company?s Domain
2. A subscription
3. A management group

Correct Answer: 3

Explanation

Since azure bills its customers per their subscription, the first thing you create in Azure is a subscription. Once a subscription has been created you can create other management tools like resource groups to group company resources, management groups for various departments and a company domain for full management of multiple accounts.

References:

- https://docs.microsoft.com/en-us/office365/enterprise/subscriptions-licensesaccounts-and-tenants-for-microsoft-cloud-offerings

Elastic computing

30. Your company owns a national wide used salary payment processing App that has very low usage on the first three weeks of the month and very high usage on the last 1 week of the month. Which benefit of Azure Cloud Services supports cost management for this type of usage pattern?

1. high availability
1. high latency
2. elasticity
3. load balancing

Correct Answer: 3

Explanation

Elastic computing is the ability to quickly expand or decrease computer processing, memory, and storage resources to meet changing demands without worrying about capacity planning and engineering for peak usage. Typically controlled by system monitoring tools, elastic computing matches the amount of resources allocated to the amount of resources actually needed without disrupting operations. With cloud elasticity, a company avoids paying for unused capacity or idle resources and doesn't have to worry about investing in the purchase or maintenance of additional resources and equipment.

References:

- https://azure.microsoft.com/en-us/overview/what-is-elastic-computing/

Cloud deployment models

31. PaaS, SaaS and IaaS are the most common cloud deployment methods used today. Which cloud deployment solution has the minimal amount of administrative effort required for services hosted on Cloud?

1. software as a service (SaaS)
1. platform as a service (PaaS)
2. infrastructure as a service (IaaS)
3. WebAPP as a service (WaaS)

Correct Answer: 1

Explanation

PaaS requires less user management. The cloud provider manages the operating systems, and the user is responsible for the applications and data they run and store SaaS requires the least amount of management. The cloud provider is responsible for managing everything, and the end user just uses the software eg Office 365 IaaS is the cloud solution with the highest administrative effort (Like virtual machines)

Reference:

- https://azure.microsoft.com/en-us/overview/what-is-paas/

Expenditure Models

32. When you plan to move your company's resources to Azure and use Pay-as-you-go subscription, which of the following expenditure model is best suited for the planned payment solution?

1. Elastic
1. Operational
2. Capital
3. Scalable
4. Cheapest

Correct Answer: 2

Explanation

The expenditure models are either CapEx (Capital) or OpEx (Operational). CapEx is what you pay upfront, on prem, for servers, racks, cooling, security, the Datacentre itself. OpEx is what you pay to keep your infrastructure operational, like IT staff. In this case, when you move to the Cloud, what you identify in this case is the OpEx or Operational model. This is because you actually don't have CapEx on the Cloud (or at least you look to minimize CapEx) as you pay for the resources you use and not for the underlying hardware, security, cooling, etc that you will pay for in an On-Prem solution. Operational. Elastic, Scalable and Cheapest are not expenditure models.

Reference:

- https://azure.microsoft.com/en-us/pricing/

Scaling

33. Azure offers dynamic scalability solutions for the services you may have hosted on their servers to ensure they can handle traffic spike and also handle low traffic without wasting resources. Which of the following 2 are the scalability types offered by Azure?

1. Elastic scaling
1. Vertical Scaling
2. Horizontal Scaling
3. Fault Scaling

Correct Answer: 2,3

Explanation

Scalability means that the servers can increase or decrease the resources and services being used based on the demand or workload. There are two types of scalability ? Vertical scaling or scaling up is the process of adding resources to increase the power of an existing server. Horizontal scaling or scaling out is the process of adding more servers that function together as one unit

Ref:

- https://docs.microsoft.com/en-us/azure/architecture/framework/scalability/design-apps

Data recovery

34. Your company hosts its customer data on Azure East US region cloud center. In the last few days the East US region has faced hurricanes that has left the datacenter where your company?s customer records were being hosted completely destroyed. Which of the following Azure solutions will be handy for the company to retrieve all lost data from Azure?

1. Fault tolerance
1. Data Recovery
2. Azure Elasticity
3. Azure Reliability

Correct Answer: 2

Explanation

Azure offers an end-to-end backup and disaster recovery solution that?s simple, secure, scalable, and cost-effective?and can be integrated with on-premises data protection solutions. In the case of service disruption or accidental deletion or corruption of data, recover your business services in a timely and orchestrated manner.

Ref:

- https://azure.microsoft.com/en-us/solutions/backup-and-disaster-recovery/

Load balancer

35. When selecting a load balancing solution for your resources hosted on Azure, which of the following are some of the things to consider?

1. Region
1. Devices used
2. Traffic type
3. Internet speed
4. Cost

Correct Answer: 1,3,5

Explanation

When selecting the load-balancing options, here are some factors to consider:

- Traffic type. Is it a web (HTTP/HTTPS) application? Is it public facing or a private application?
- Global versus. regional. Do you need to load balance VMs or containers within a virtual network, or load balance scale unit/deployments across regions, or both?
- Availability. What is the service SLA for your resources?
- Cost. See Azure pricing. In addition to the cost of the service itself, consider the operations cost for managing a solution built on that service.
- Features and limits. What are the overall limitations of each service? See Service limits.

Ref:

- https://docs.microsoft.com/en-us/azure/architecture/guide/technology-choices/load-balancing-overview

Management groups

36. If your company owns multiple Azure subscriptions, which is the way to efficiently manage access, policies, and compliance for those subscriptions?

1. Have a single resource group
1. Have a single management group
2. Delete all those subscriptions and leave one
3. Join all those subscriptions into one

Correct Answer: 2

Explanation

Azure management groups provide a level of scope above subscriptions. You organize subscriptions into containers called management groups and apply your governance conditions to the management groups. All subscriptions within a management group automatically inherit the conditions applied to the management group

Ref:

- https://docs.microsoft.com/en-us/learn/modules/azure-architecture-fundamentals/management-groups-subscriptions

37. Your company has one management group that contains multiple subscriptions. Each subscription have multiple resources groups within them. You need to implement an Azure policy that Virtual Machines should only be created in one region. Which is the most efficient level to implement the policy?

1. The resource groups
1. The subscription

2. The Management Group

3. All the levels

Correct Answer: 3

Explanation

You can apply policies to a management group that limits the regions available for VM creation. This policy would be applied to all management groups, subscriptions, and resources under that management group by only allowing VMs to be created in that region.

Ref:

- https://docs.microsoft.com/en-us/learn/modules/azure-architecture-fundamentals/management-groups-subscriptions

38. which of the following facts is/are FALSE about the management groups in Azure Directory?

1. 1,000,000 management groups can be supported in a single directory.
1. Each management group and subscription can support only one parent.
2. All subscriptions and management groups are within a single hierarchy in each directory.
3. Management groups can share a directory.
4. Each management group can have many children.

Correct Answer: 1,4

Explanation

Facts about management Groups are:

- 10,000 management groups can be supported in a single directory.

- A management group tree can support up to six levels of depth. This limit doesn't include the root level or the subscription level.
- Each management group and subscription can support only one parent.
  - Each management group can have many children.
  - All subscriptions and management groups are within a single hierarchy in each directory.

Ref:

- https://docs.microsoft.com/en-us/learn/modules/azure-architecture-fundamentals/management-groups-subscriptions

39. What happens when you delete a resource group that contains VMs, storage account and Database?

1. Only the Resource group is deleted but the rest of resources remains
1. VMs and Database are deleted but storage account is left
2. VMs are not deleted but the rest of resources are deleted.
3. Everything is deleted including the resource group.

Correct Answer: 4

Explanation

If you delete a resource group, all resources contained within it are also deleted. Organizing resources by life cycle can be useful in nonproduction environments, where you might try an experiment and then dispose of it. Resource groups make it easy to remove a set of resources all at once.

Ref:

- https://docs.microsoft.com/en-us/learn/modules/azure-architecture-fundamentals/resources-resource-manager

40. Rather than dealing with resources individually, Azure Resource manager helps you automate some of the tasks. Which of the following tasks is NOT performed by a Resource manager?

1. Deploy
1. Test
2. Monitor
3. Manage

Correct Answer: 2

Explanation

With Resource Manager, you can:

- Manage your infrastructure through declarative templates rather than scripts. A Resource Manager template is a JSON file that defines what you want to deploy to Azure.
- Deploy, manage, and monitor all the resources for your solution as a group, rather than handling these resources individually.
- Redeploy your solution throughout the development life cycle and have confidence your resources are deployed in a consistent state.

Ref:

- https://docs.microsoft.com/en-us/learn/modules/azure-architecture-fundamentals/resources-resource-manager

41. Which of the following can be used to manage governance across multiple Azure subscriptions?

1. Resources
1. Resource Group
2. management Group
3. Resources Manager

Correct Answer: 3

Explanation

Management groups facilitate the hierarchical ordering of Azure resources into collections, at a level of scope above subscriptions. Distinct governance conditions can be applied to each management group, with Azure Policy and Azure role-based access controls, to manage Azure subscriptions effectively. The resources and subscriptions assigned to a management group automatically inherit the conditions applied to the management group.

REF:

- https://docs.microsoft.com/en-us/azure/governance/management-groups/overview

42. Which of the following statements is correct about Root Management Group in Azure?

1. root management group can't be moved or deleted
1. 'All customers can see and have access to manage root management group.
2. All subscriptions and management groups fold up to the one root management group   within the directory.
3. New subscriptions have to be added to the root management group when created manually.

Correct Answer: 1,3

Explanation

Each directory is given a single top-level management group called the "Root" management group. This root management group is built into the hierarchy to have all management groups and subscriptions fold up to it. This root management group allows for global policies and Azure role assignments to be applied at the directory level. The Azure AD Global Administrator needs to elevate themselves to the User Access Administrator role of this root group initially. After elevating access, the administrator can assign any Azure role to other directory users or groups to manage the hierarchy. As administrator, you can assign your own account as owner of the root management group.

REF:

- https://docs.microsoft.com/en-us/azure/governance/management-groups/overview

Azure Regions

43. Every Azure region has multiple data center. Is this statement correct?

1. TRUE
1. FALSE

Correct Answer: 1

Explanation

A region is a set of datacenters deployed within a latency-defined perimeter and connected through a dedicated regional low-latency network. Azure intelligently assigns and controls the resources within each region to ensure workloads are appropriately balanced. When you deploy a resource in Azure, you'll often need to choose the region where you want your resource deployed.

Ref:

- https://docs.microsoft.com/en-us/learn/modules/azure-architecture-fundamentals/regions-availability-zones

44. Which of the following Azure region are NOT open to public companies of people residing in United States?

1. Azure North Europe
1. Azure West US 2
2. Azure Central US
3. Azure DoD Central US

Correct Answer: 4

Explanation

US DoD Central, US Gov Virginia, US Gov Iowa etc are regions with physical and logical network-isolated instances of Azure for U.S. government agencies and partners. These datacenters are operated by screened U.S. personnel and include additional compliance certifications and hence not open to public.

Ref:

- https://azure.microsoft.com/en-us/global-infrastructure/government/

Availability Zones

45. What do we call a physically separate datacenters within an Azure region. made up of one or more datacenters that ensure your services and data are redundant so you can protect your information in case of failure?

1. A scale set
1. An Azure region
2. Availability zone
3. Fault tolerance

Correct Answer: 3

Explanation

availability zones to run mission-critical applications and build high-availability into your application architecture by co-locating your compute, storage, networking, and data resources within a zone and replicating in other zones.

Ref:

- https://azure.microsoft.com/en-us/global-infrastructure/availability-zones/

46. Availability zones are primarily for VMs, managed disks, load balancers, and SQL databases. Azure services that support availability zones fall into two categories: Zonal services and Zonal redundant services. Which of the Azure services listed above support Zonal redundant services?

1. VMs
1. Managed disks
2. Load balancers

3. SQL databases

Correct Answer: 4

Explanation

Zone-redundant services the platform replicates automatically across zones for example, zone-redundant storage, SQL Database. Zonal services pins the resource to a specific zone for example, VMs, managed disks, IP addresses.

Ref:

- https://docs.microsoft.com/en-us/learn/modules/azure-architecture-fundamentals/regions-availability-zones

47. All Microsoft Azure regions worldwide support availability zones. Is this statement correct?

1. TRUE
1. FALSE

Correct Answer: 2

Explanation

Availability zones aren?t available in all Azure regions, nor are they available for all Azure services in regions that support them.

Ref:

- https://docs.microsoft.com/en-us/azure/availability-zones/az-overview

Azure region pairs

48. What is meant by an Azure Region Pair?

1. An Azure region paired with another Azure region within the same geography
1. An Azure Datacenter paired with another Datacenter within the same region to create a pair
2. Multiple Azure regions connected by a low latency network
3. Azure regions in the same country or block

Correct Answer: 1

Explanation

An Azure region consists of a set of data centres deployed within a latency-defined perimeter and connected through a dedicated low-latency network. This ensures that Azure services within an Azure region offer the best possible performance and security. An Azure geography defines an area of the world containing at least one Azure region. Geographies define a discrete market, typically containing two or more regions, that preserve data residency and compliance boundaries.

Ref:

- https://docs.microsoft.com/en-us/azure/best-practices-availability-paired-regions

49. You have been provided with the following Azure regions across the globe :Canada Central ,China East, China North, Canada East, West India, South India, West Us and UK East. Which of the following is not a valid Azure region pair from the provided list?

1. West India & South India
1. Canada Central & Canada East

2. West US and UK East

3. China North & China East

Correct Answer: 3

Explanation

A regional pair consists of two regions within the same geography and usually 300miles or less from each other. West Us and UK East regions are over 1000 miles apart hence cannot make a reginal pair.

Ref:

- https://docs.microsoft.com/en-us/azure/best-practices-availability-paired-regions

50. Which of the following statements describes an advantage of a Azure regional pair ?

1. If an extensive Azure outage occurs, one region out of every pair is prioritized to make sure at least one is restored as quickly as possible for applications hosted in that region pair.

1. Planned Azure updates are rolled out to paired regions one region at a time to minimize downtime and risk of application outage.

2. Data continues to reside within the same geography as its pair (except for Brazil South) for tax- and law-enforcement jurisdiction purposes.

3. All of the above.

Correct Answer: 4

Explanation

Because the pair of regions is directly connected and far enough apart to be isolated from regional disasters, you can use them to provide reliable services and data redundancy. Some services offer automatic geo-redundant storage by using region pairs.

Ref:

- https://docs.microsoft.com/en-us/learn/modules/azure-architecture-fundamentals/regions-availability-zones

App services

51. What is Azure App service?

1. Application that can be hosted in Azure cloud
1. An Azure environment to deploy and test your applications
2. HTTP-based service that enables you to build and host many types of web-based solutions without managing infrastructure
3. An application developed in Azure without coding and infrastructure

Correct Answer: 3

Explanation

App Service is an HTTP-based service that enables you to build and host many types of web-based solutions without managing infrastructure. For example, you can host web apps, mobile back ends, and RESTful APIs in several supported programming languages. Applications developed in .NET, .NET Core, Java, Ruby, Node.js, PHP, or Python can run in and scale with ease on both Windows- and Linux-based environments.

Ref:

- https://azure.microsoft.com/en-us/services/app-service/

Locks

52. You have created a resource group and added a delete Lock on it. Later one your workmate creates a VM with a blob storage attached in the same resource group but he is unable to delete the VM after using it. What should your workmate do?

1. Just leave the VM running
1. Deallocate VM and leave it that way
2. Notify you to remove all lock applied to the Resource Group
3. Delete the management group that has the VMS

Correct Answer: 3

Explanation

Leaving the VM running will continue to generate charges and deallocating it with storage account attached also generate storage account charges. Deleting A management group may have a catastrophic consequence as it deleted all other subscriptions and resource groups.

PART 3

Describe Core Azure Services

Reginal Pairs

1. When You deploy resources in Azure in you can choose the region and regional pair your resources will be deployed. Is this statement correct?

1. TRUE
1. FALSE

Correct Answer: 2

Explanation

Even though you can choose the region where Azure should deploy your resources you cannot choose the regional pare that your data will be kept to cushion against catastrophic events that may affect a region.

Reference:

- https://docs.microsoft.com/en-us/azure/best-practices-availability-paired-regions

Azure Portal

2. Microsoft Azure main dashboard is stored as what type of file?

1. XML
1. JSON
2. DOCX
3. HTML

Correct Answer: 2

Explanation

Azure dashboard is stored in JSON file format which can easily be downloaded or uploaded and shared with other Azure directories you have. Those JSON files are editable and are made of properties like the Azure resource ID, Name, Type, Location and Tags.

Ref:

- https://docs.microsoft.com/en-us/azure/azure-portal/azure-portal-dashboards-structure

3. You have an Azure environment that contains your company's Azure resources. To which URL should you connect to directly to this resource?

1. https://portal.microsoftazure.com
1. https://portal.azure.com
2. https://portal.microsoft.com
3. htps://azure.microsoft.com/portal

Correct Answer: 2

Explanation

- https://portal.azure.com > This the Azure portal direct link to the resources, dashboard and the marketplace and dashboard

Azure Regions

4. Deploying an App on Azure can be done directly to what level of physical Granularity?

1. Servers
1. Server Rack
2. Data center
3. Region

Correct Answer: 4

Explanation

Microsoft Azure always organises its resources into regions that are made of datacenters, deployed within a latency-defined perimeter and connected through a dedicated regional low-latency network. You can pick the region you want your services to be deployed into but you cannot pick the Datacenter, servers or server racks where they will be deployed.

Ref:

- https://azure.microsoft.com/en-us/global-infrastructure/

Storage services

5. You work for US based company that saves a huge amount of data and files regarding its projects. The company plans on using Azure Storage account to store 2TB of Data and a million files. Does Azure storage meet these requirements?

1. TRUE
1. FALSE

Correct Answer: 1

Explanation

The current storage limit is 2 PB for US and Europe, and 500 TB for all other regions (including the UK) with no limit on the number of files that can be stored in an azure storage account.

Ref:

- https://docs.microsoft.com/en-us/azure/storage/common/scalability-targets-standard-account

6. Which of the following storage service is used to store the unmanaged data disks of the virtual machine that you have created in Azure?

1. Containers/Blobs
1. File Shares
2. Tables
3. Queues

Correct Answer: 1

Explanation

Containers/Blobs: REST-based object storage for unstructured data.

File Shares: File shares that use the standard SMB 3.0 protocol.

Tables: Tabular data storage.

Queues: Effectively scale apps according to traffic.

REF:

- https://docs.microsoft.com/en-us/azure/storage/blobs/storage-blobs-introduction

Scale sets

7. Your Company plans to deploy several apps that are accessed by customers consistently on Azure Virtual Machines. Due to the high app usage and demand from customers you need to ensure that their services are available even when a single Datacenter that hosts the virtual machines fails. You resolve to deploy the virtual machines to two or more scale sets. Does this meet the goal?

1. Yes
1. No

Correct Answer: 1

Explanation

Scale sets provide high availability to your applications, and allow you to centrally manage, configure, and update a large number of VMs. With virtual machine scale sets, you can build large-scale services for areas such as compute, big data, and container workloads. The number of VM instances can automatically increase or decrease in response to demand or a defined schedule workload. The number of VM instances can automatically increase or decrease in response to demand or a defined schedule.

Reference.

- https://azure.microsoft.com/en-us/services/virtual-machine-scale-sets/

Availability Zones

8. Which type failure can be protected by Azure Availability Zone?

1. a physical server failure
1. an Azure region failure
2. a storage failure
3. an Azure data center failure

Correct Answer: 4

Explanation

Availability zones expand the level of control you have to maintain the availability of the applications and data on your VMs. An Availability Zone is a physically separate zone, within an Azure region. There are three Availability Zones per supported Azure region. Each Availability Zone has a distinct power source, network, and cooling. By architecting your solutions to use replicated VMs in zones, you can protect your apps and data from the loss of a datacenter. If one zone is compromised, then replicated apps and data are instantly available in another zone.

Ref:

- https://docs.microsoft.com/en-us/azure/availability-zones/az-overview

Azure Monitor

9. Which of the following Azure service should you use from the Azure portal to view service failure notifications that can affect the availability of an Azure Virtual Machine?

1. Azure Service Fabric
1. Azure Monitor
2. Azure virtual machines
3. Azure Advisor

Correct Answer: 5

Explanation

Azure Monitor maximizes the availability and performance of your applications by delivering a comprehensive solution for collecting, analysing, and acting on telemetry from your cloud and on-premises environments. It helps you understand how your applications are performing and proactively identifies issues affecting them and the resources they depend on. All data collected by Azure Monitor fits into one of two fundamental types, metrics and logs. Metrics are numerical values that describe some aspect of a system at a particular point in time. They are lightweight and capable of supporting near real-time scenarios. Logs contain different kinds of data organized into records with different sets of properties for each type. Telemetry such as events and traces are stored as logs in addition to performance data so that it can all be combined for analysis.

Ref:

- https://docs.microsoft.com/en-us/azure/azure-monitor/overview

Azure CLI

10. Which of the following tools can you use to run Azure CLI?

1. Command Prompt
1. Azure File Explorer
2. Azure Resources Explorer
3. Windows PowerShell
4. Microsoft Directory

Correct Answer: 1,4

Explanation

The Azure CLI is a command-line tool providing a great experience for managing Azure resources. The CLI is designed to make scripting easy, query data, support long-running operations, and more. For Windows the Azure CLI is installed via an MSI, which gives you access to the CLI through the Windows Command Prompt (CMD) or PowerShell. When installing for Windows Subsystem for Linux (WSL), packages are available for your Linux distribution.

Ref:

- https://docs.microsoft.com/en-us/cli/azure/install-azure-cli-windows?view=azure-cli-latest&tabs=azure-cli

11. As an administrator, you need to retrieve the IP address from a particular VM by using Bash. Which of the following tools should you use?

1. ARM templates
1. Azure PowerShell
2. The Azure portal
3. The Azure CLI

Explanation

enables you to use Bash to run one-off tasks on Azure. The Azure command-line interface (Azure CLI) is a set of commands used to create and manage Azure resources. The Azure CLI is available across Azure services and is designed to get you working quickly with Azure, with an emphasis on automation.

Ref:

- https://docs.microsoft.com/en-us/cli/azure/

Azure File service

12. You have several Computers in your workplace running Windows 10 Operating system. You need to map a network drive from the computers to Azure storage. What solution should you create on Azure to enable the mapping?

1. an Azure SQL database
1. a virtual machine data disk
2. a Files service in a storage account
3. a Blobs service in a storage account

Correct Answer: 3

Explanation

Azure Files offers fully managed file shares in the cloud that are accessible via the industry standard Server Message Block (SMB) protocol. Azure file shares can be mounted concurrently by cloud or on-premises deployments of Windows, Linux, and macOS. Additionally, Azure file shares can be cached on Windows Servers with Azure File Sync for fast access near where the data is being used.

Ref:

- https://docs.microsoft.com/en-us/azure/storage/files/storage-how-to-use-files-windows

Azure CDN

13. You have a Movies and Music streaming website hosting large video and audio files, accessed my people worldwide and its hosted on your local server. You plan to expand to Azure cloud. Which Azure feature must be used to provide the best video playback experience?

1. an application gateway
1. an Azure ExpressRoute circuit
2. a content delivery network (CDN)
3. an Azure Traffic Manager profile

Correct Answer: 3

Explanation

A CDN is a distributed network of server that can efficiently deliver high quality web content to user like Vimeo or YouTube. With Azure CDN, you can cache static objects loaded from Azure Blob storage, a web application, or any publicly accessible web server, by using the closest point of presence (POP) server. Azure CDN can also accelerate dynamic content, which cannot be cached, by leveraging various network and routing optimizations.

Ref:

- https://docs.microsoft.com/en-us/azure/cdn/

Azure IoT Hub

14. Which Azure resources could you use with a Hub made of several millions of home sensors that will upload data for analysis and storage in Azure?

1. Azure Data Lake
1. Azure Queue storage
2. Azure File Storage
3. Azure IoT Hubs
4. Azure Notification Hubs

Correct Answer: 1,4

Explanation

There are two storage services IoT Hub can route messages to ' Azure Blob Storage and Azure Data Lake Storage Gen2 (ADLS Gen2) accounts. Azure Data Lake Storage accounts are hierarchical namespace-enabled storage accounts built on top of blob storage. Both of these use blobs for their storage.

Ref:

- https://docs.microsoft.com/en-us/azure/iot-hub/iot-hub-devguide-messages-d2c

Azure resources

15. Your company has an on-premises network that contains multiple servers. The company plans to reduce the following administrative responsibilities of network administrators. The company plans to migrate several servers to Azure virtual machines. Which administrative responsibilities will be reduced after the planned migration?

1. Replacing failed server hardware
1. Backing up application data
2. Managing physical server security
3. Updating server operating systems
4. Managing permissions to shared documents

Correct Answer: 1,3

Explanation

A. Replacing failed server hardware - so no more PHYSICAL hardware to replace

C. Managing physical server security - No PHYSICAL servers, No PHYSICAL security to care about.

incorrect:

B. Backing up application data - you'll still need to backup app data

D. Updating server operating systems - VM OS still need to be updated...

E. Managing permissions to shared documents - Also this still need to be managed.

Ref:

- https://azure.microsoft.com/en-us/migration/migration-journey/#how-to-migrate

Azure Management tools

16. Which of the following Azure Management tools could you use to manage settings of a Web app you have hosted on Azure using only your iPhone Smartphone?

1. Azure CLI
1. the Azure portal
2. Azure Cloud Shell
3. Windows PowerShell
4. Azure Storage Explorer

Correct Answer: 2,3

Explanation

Azure Command Line Interface cannot be installed on iPhone's IOS. Windows PowerShell also cannot be installed on iPhone's IOS. Azure Storage Explorer couldn't be use to manage web apps settings or another azure resource. Therefore, the only tools that can we use to managed web apps settings from an iPhone is the Azure Portal and Azure Cloud Shell through a browser. Another way to run the settings from iPhone is through Azure portal app.

Ref:

- http://www.deployazure.com/management/managing-azure-from-ipad/

Serverless Computing

17. You company owns a short video and photo sharing application that runs on millions of smartphones worldwide. The demand and usage are highly unpredictable but there is always a traffic spike when a worldwide or national significant event occurs. Which Azure compute services is best suited for this kind of unpredictable workload?

1. Azure Virtual Machines
1. Azure Machine Learning
2. Azure IoT Hub
3. Azure Serverless Computing

Correct Answer: 4

Explanation

The app is event driven and it needs to handle unpredictable demand from events. Azure Serverless computing enables Dynamic Scalability to handle spike in traffic and scale down resources when there is no significant event. This method is cost effective for the company as you pay for resources only used.

Ref:

- https://azure.microsoft.com/en-us/overview/serverless-computing/

Scale sets

18. You Company plan to deploy several Azure virtual machines and ensure that the services running on the virtual machines are available if a single data centre fails. Which of the solutions listed below best meets the goal?

1. Deploy the VMs in an Azure datacentre closest to your company.
1. Deploy the VMs in multiple company subscriptions.
2. Deploy the VMs in two or more scale sets.
3. Deploy the VMs into 2 or more availability sets.

Correct Answer: 3

Explanation

Azure virtual machine scale sets let you create and manage a group of identical, load balanced VMs. The number of VM instances can automatically increase or decrease in response to demand or a defined schedule. Scale sets provide high availability to your applications, and allow you to centrally manage, configure, and update a large number of VMs. With virtual machine scale sets, you can build large-scale services for areas such as compute, big data, and container workloads.

References:

- https://azure.microsoft.com/en-us/services/virtual-machine-scale-sets/

Database services

19. What is the major advantage of Azure SQL for Database?

1. Its supports Automatic Scaling
1. Has Data compression capabilities for storage optimization
2. Has inbuilt high Availability
3. Supports millions of files

Correct Answer: 3

Explanation

SQL Data Warehouse is supported by a broad ecosystem of partners, including data preparation, ingestion service and visualisation tool providers. Enjoy guaranteed 99.9 percent availability in all Azure regions worldwide.

Ref:

- https://azure.microsoft.com/en-us/resources/videos/introduction-to-azure-sql-data-warehouse/#:~:text=Azure%20SQL%20Data%20Warehouse%20is,%2Das%2Dyou%20go%20environment.

Azure Advisor

20. Your company has an Azure subscription that contains the following unused resources:
20 user accounts in Azure Active Directory (Azure AD).
Five groups in Azure AD.
10 public IP addresses.
10 network interfaces.
You need to reduce the Azure costs for the company. Which of the following solution meets this goal?

1. Remove User accounts from Azure AD
1. Delete all groups in Azure AD
2. Delete all public Ip addresses
3. Remove all network interfaces

Correct Answer: 3

Explanation

public IP addresses that are not currently associated to Azure resources such as Load Balancers or VMs. These public IP addresses come with a nominal charge. If you do not plan to use them, deleting them can result in cost savings

Ref:

- https://docs.microsoft.com/en-us/azure/advisor/advisor-cost-recommendations#delete-unassociated-public-ip-addresses-to-save-money

Azure Resource Manager

21. Does Creating additional resource groups in an Azure subscription incur additional costs?

1. Yes
1. No

Correct Answer: 2

Explanation

> adding resource groups generates no extra cost in Azure. Only when resources that have cost value are added to those resources will the cost be incurred.

REF:

- https://docs.microsoft.com/en-us/azure/azure-resource-manager/templates/deploy-portal

22. Can a resource group can contain resources from multiple Azure regions?

1. TRUE
1. FALSE

Correct Answer: 1

Explanation

Resources from multiple different regions can be placed in a resource group.

The resource group only contains metadata about the resources it contains.

REF:

- https://docs.microsoft.com/en-us/azure/azure-resource-manager/templates/deploy-to-resource-group?tabs=azure-cli

Azure Pricing

23. Your company needs to copy 500 GBs of data from local network server to an Azure storage via a VPN they have. The is no extra charges incurred since Azure does not charge inbound traffic. Is this correct?

1. TRUE
1. False

Correct Answer: 2

Explanation

Data transfers between two virtual networks are charged at the Inter-virtual network rates noted above. Other data transfers over the VPN connections to your on-premises sites or the internet in general are charged separately at the regular data transfer rate

REF:

- https://azure.microsoft.com/en-us/pricing/details/vpn-gateway/

Storage Redundancy Services

24. Which of the following is TRUE about all data that is copied to an Azure Storage account

1. It is backed up automatically to another Azure data center.
1. Data is replicated asynchronously three times in the primary region
2. Data'replicated asynchronously to the secondary region
3. Geo-redundant storage (GRS) has cross-regional replication to protect against regional outages

Correct Answer: 4

Explanation

Data is not backed up automatically to another Azure Data Center although it can be depending on the replication option configured for the account. Geo-redundant storage (GRS) has cross-regional replication to protect against regional outages. Data is replicated synchronously three times in the primary region, then replicated asynchronously to the secondary region.

Ref:

- https://docs.microsoft.com/en-us/azure/storage/common/storage-redundancy

25. In how many copies does Locally Redundant Storage replicated your data across physical locations?

1. 1
1. 2
2. 6
3. 3

Correct Answer: 4

Explanation

Locally redundant storage (LRS) replicates your data three times within a single physical location in the primary region. LRS provides at least 99.999999999% (11 nines) durability of objects over a given year. LRS is the lowest-cost redundancy option and offers the least durability compared to other options. LRS protects your data against server rack and drive failures.

REF:

- https://docs.microsoft.com/en-us/azure/storage/common/storage-redundancy

26. If flooding or fire occurs in an Azure datacenter, which of the following storage redundancy solutions will not protect your data from damage caused by such events?

1. Zone redundant storage (ZRS)
1. Locally redundant storage (LRS)
2. Geo redundant storage (ZRS)
3. Geo-Zone redundant storage (GZRS)

Correct Answer: 2

Explanation

LRS is the lowest-cost redundancy option and offers the least durability compared to other options. LRS protects your data against server rack and drive failures. However, if a disaster such as fire or flooding occurs within the data center, all replicas of a storage account using LRS may be lost or unrecoverable. To mitigate this risk, Microsoft recommends using zone-redundant storage (ZRS), geo-redundant storage (GRS), or geo-zone-redundant storage (GZRS).

REF:

- https://docs.microsoft.com/en-us/azure/storage/common/storage-redundancy

27. You company owns an application that restricts data replication over an Azure region/country due Governance requirement. You need to choose the best storage redundancy solution for your company. Which of the following will you choose?

1. Zone redundant storage (ZRS)
1. Locally redundant storage (LRS)
2. Geo redundant storage (ZRS)
3. Geo-Zone redundant storage (GZRS)

Correct Answer: 2

Explanation

LRS replicates your data three times within a single physical location in the primary region and hence no data is backed up on other regions or countries ensuring it conforms the set governance requirements.

Ref:

- https://docs.microsoft.com/en-us/azure/storage/common/storage-redundancy

28. How many copies of your data are does Azure have globally when you choose to use Geo redundant Storage (GRS)?

1. 2
1. 3
2. 4
3. 6

Correct Answer: 3

Explanation

Geo-redundant storage (GRS) copies your data synchronously three times within a single physical location in the primary region using LRS. It then copies your data asynchronously to a single physical location in the secondary region.

Ref:

- https://docs.microsoft.com/en-us/azure/storage/common/storage-redundancy

29. Which of the following functions you cannot automatically perform to your data in secondary region if you choose Geo redundant storage (ZRS) or Geo-Zone redundant storage (GZRS)?

1. Delete
1. Read
2. Backup
3. Write
4. Sync

Correct Answer: 2,4

Explanation

> With GRS or GZRS, the data in the secondary region isn't available for read or write access unless there is a failover to the secondary region. For read access to the secondary region, configure your storage account to use read-access geo-redundant storage (RA-GRS) or read-access geo-zone-redundant storage (RA-GZRS).

Ref:

- https://docs.microsoft.com/en-us/azure/storage/common/storage-redundancy#read-access-to-data-in-the-secondary-region

Azure Websites

30. You have a publicly accessible website hosted in your local network. You plan to move the website to azure due to unpredictable traffic spike. Which of the following statement is true about movie the site to Azure?

1. You must use a VPN to move web files from local to Azure.
   1. B. You must pay to transfer the site to Azure
2. C. Once the site is set up on Azure you will incur some monthly charges
3. D. The number of connections will be reduced once the app goes live on Azure

Correct Answer: 3

Explanation

When planning to migrate a public website to Azure, you must plan to pay monthly usage costs. This is because Azure uses the pay-as-you-go mode that charges for all the resources that the website will be using including services such as storage and database.

Ref:

- https://azure.microsoft.com/en-us/blog/how-to-plan-your-migration-to-azure-websites/

Azure Subscription

31. Which Azure platform that provides a platform for deploying objects to a cloud infrastructure and for implementing consistency across the Azure environment.

1. multiple subscriptions
1. multiple Azure Active Directory (Azure AD) directories
2. multiple regions
3. multiple resource groups

Correct Answer: 1

Explanation

A subscription is an agreement with Microsoft to use one or more Microsoft cloud platforms or services, for which charges accrue based on either a per-user license fee or on cloud-based resource consumption. It enables segmentation of departments costs hence there is no mix up.

Ref:

- https://docs.microsoft.com/en-us/microsoft-365/enterprise/subscriptions-licenses-accounts-and-tenants-for-microsoft-cloud-offerings?view=o365-worldwide

Azure Cloud Shell

32. You are way away from your workstation and your workmates calls and tells you they need you to create an Azure VM instantly to be used for testing purposes. You only have your Android OS tablet with you. Which of the following tools could you use on Android tablet to create the VM?

1. PowerShell In Azure Cloud shell
1. Command prompt
2. Azure mobile App
3. Windows PowerShell
4. Bash in Cloud Shell

Correct Answer: 1,3,5

Explanation

Azure Cloud Shell can be used for Bash or PowerShell, either Android Phone or Laptop and can be virtually executed everywhere.

REF:

- https://docs.microsoft.com/en-us/azure/cloud-shell/overview

Azure Database

33. You plan to implement an Azure database solution that can add data concurrently from multiple regions and Can store JSON documents. Which database service should you deploy?

1. Azure Cosmos DB.
1. Azure Database for MySQL servers.
2. SQL Servers.
3. SQL data warehouse.
4. Azure Database for PostgreSQL servers

Correct Answer: 1

Explanation

Azure Cosmos DB is Microsoft's globally distributed, multi-model database service. With a click of a button, Cosmos DB enables you to elastically and independently scale throughput and storage across any number of Azure regions worldwide. You can elastically scale throughput and storage, and take advantage of fast, single-digit-millisecond data access using your favourite API including: SQL, MongoDB, Cassandra, Tables, or Gremlin. Cosmos DB provides comprehensive service level agreements (SLAs) for throughput, latency, availability, and consistency guarantees, something no other database service offers.

Ref:

- https://docs.microsoft.com/en-us/azure/cosmos-db/introduction

Azure support

34. What the following feature/service is guaranteed in an Azure Service Level Agreement (SLA)?

1. Performance
1. Feature Availability
2. Dynamic Elasticity
3. Uptime

Correct Answer: 2

Explanation

Azure guarantee at least 99.9% availability of: Azure AD, App services, Azure Advisor, Azure Analysis etc

REF:

- https://azure.microsoft.com/en-us/support/legal/sla/summary/

Azure Product Status

35. What does it mean when Azure releases a product in public review?

1. Service is in public beta and can be tried out by anyone with an Azure subscription.
1. The product is being offered free of charge for everything
2. The product can be used outside Azure environment
3. The product is open-source so therefore can be used by the public

Correct Answer: 1

Explanation

Product in public review means that it maybe be used by all Azure customers with a subscription. The product is usually provided at highly discounted prices to attract more customers.

REF:

- https://azure.microsoft.com/en-us/updates/?status=InPreview

36. Azure services are usually released in phases. Which of the options notes the correct phase of releasing Azure resources for public use?

1. Private preview 'Public preview 'general availability
1. general availability' Private preview 'Public preview
2. Public preview 'general availability' Private preview
3. Private preview 'general availability 'Public preview

Correct Answer: 1

Explanation

Most services go to private preview then public preview before being released to general availability. The private preview is only available to certain Azure customers for evaluation purposes. The public preview is available to all Azure customers.

REF:

- https://azure-overview.com/Home/Faq

Azure Repos

37. Which Azure service provides a set of version control tools to manage code?

1. Azure Repos
1. Azure DevTest Labs
2. Azure Storage
3. Azure Cosmos DB

Correct Answer: 1

Explanation

> Azure Repos is a set of version control tools that you can use to manage your code.

Azure DevTest Labs creates labs consisting of pre-configured bases or Azure Resource Manager templates. These have all the necessary tools and software that you can use to create environments.

Azure Cosmos DB is Microsoft's globally distributed, multi-model database service.

REF:

- https://docs.microsoft.com/en-us/azure/devops/repos/get-started/what-is-repos?view=azure-devops

Azure Functions

38. Which of the following services provided by Azure that enables Serverless Computing?

1. Azure Virtual Machines
1. Azure Functions
2. Azure storage account
3. Azure Container Instances

Correct Answer: 1

Explanation

Azure Functions provide a platform for serverless code. Azure Functions is a serverless compute service that lets you run event-triggered code without having to explicitly provision or manage infrastructure.

REF:

- https://docs.microsoft.com/en-us/azure/azure-functions/

Azure Accounts

39. Your company recently moved into using Azure services and its on free subscription account. This means that you are only exposed to a subset of Azure resources. IS this statement correct?

1. TRUE
1. FALSE

Correct Answer: 2

Explanation

Azure Free Account gives you 12 months access to the most popular free services. It also gives you a credit (150 GBP or 200 USD) to use on any Azure service for up to 30 days.

Ref:

- https://azure.microsoft.com/en-us/free/free-account-faq/

Storage Accounts

40. What is the first step that you would take in order to share an image file as a blob in Azure Storage?

1. Create an Azure Storage container to store the image.
1. Create an Azure Storage account.
2. Upload the image file and create a container.
3. Use a Shared Access Signature (SAS) token to restrict access to the image.

Correct Answer: 2

Explanation

You must create an Azure Storage account before you can use any Azure Storage features.

Reference:

- https://docs.microsoft.com/en-us/azure/storage/common/storage-account-overview

41. Which Azure Storage option is better for storing data for backup and restore, disaster recovery, and archiving?

1. Azure Files Storage
1. Azure Disk Storage
2. Azure Blob Storage

Correct Answer: 3

Explanation

Azure Blob Storage is your best option for storing disaster recovery files and archives.

Reference:

- https://docs.microsoft.com/en-us/azure/storage/common/storage-account-overview

Virtual Networks

42. Azure virtual networks enable you to link resources together in your on-premises environment and within your Azure subscription. There are mechanisms for you to achieve this connectivity, EXCEPT which one?

1. Azure ExpressRoute
1. Point-to-site Virtual private Network
2. Site-to-site virtual private Network
3. Network Virtual Appliance

Correct Answer: 4

Explanation

A network virtual appliance is a specialized VM that can be compared to a hardened network appliance. A network virtual appliance carries out a particular network function, such as running a firewall or performing wide area network (WAN) optimization. Its therefore not a mechanism for Azure VN to connect with local on-premises network.

Ref:

- https://docs.microsoft.com/en-us/learn/modules/azure-networking-fundamentals/azure-virtual-network-fundamentals

43. Which of the following options can you use to link virtual networks?

1. Network address translation
1. Multi-chassis link aggregation
2. Dynamic Host Configuration Protocol
3. Virtual network peering

Correct Answer: 4

Explanation

Virtual network peering can be used to link virtual networks. Virtual network peering enables you to seamlessly connect two or more Virtual Networks in Azure. The virtual networks appear as one for connectivity purposes. The traffic between virtual machines in peered virtual networks uses the Microsoft backbone infrastructure. Like traffic between virtual machines in the same network, traffic is routed through Microsoft's private network only.

Reference:

- https://docs.microsoft.com/en-us/azure/virtual-network/virtual-network-peering-overview

Azure Networks

44. Your Company wants to create a secure communication tunnel between its branch offices. Which of the following technologies can't be used?

1. Point-to-site virtual private network
1. Implicit FTP over SSL
2. Azure ExpressRoute
3. Site-to-site virtual private network

Correct Answer: 2

Explanation

FTP over SSL can't be used to create a secure communication tunnel.Unlike using HTTP over SSL, which requires a separate port and connection for secure (HTTPS) communication, secure FTP communication occurs on the same port as non-secure communication.

Reference:

- https://docs.microsoft.com/en-us/iis/configuration/system.applicationhost/sites/site/ftpserver/security/ssl

45. Your company wants to use Azure ExpressRoute to connect its on-premises network to the Microsoft cloud. Which of the following choices isn't an ExpressRoute model that you can use?

1. Any-to-any connection
1. Site-to-site virtual private network
2. Point-to-point Ethernet connection
3. Cloud Exchange colocation

Explanation

A site-to-site virtual private network isn't an ExpressRoute model.You can create a connection between your on-premises network and the Microsoft cloud in four different ways, CloudExchange Co-location, Point-to-point Ethernet Connection, Any-to-any (IPVPN) Connection, and ExpressRoute Direct. Connectivity providers may offer one or more connectivity models.

Reference:

- https://docs.microsoft.com/en-us/azure/expressroute/expressroute-connectivity-models

46. Azure Networks

1. a virtual network gateway
   1. a load balancer
2. an application gateway
3. a virtual network
4. a gateway subnet

Correct Answer: 1,5

Explanation

To implement a solution that enables the client computers on your on-premises network to communicate to the Azure virtual machines, you need to configure a VPN (Virtual Private Network) to connect the on-premises network to the Azure virtual network. The Azure VPN device is known as a Virtual Network Gateway. The virtual network gateway needs to be located in a dedicated subnet in the Azure virtual network. This dedicated subnet is known as a gateway subnet and must be named 'Gateway Subnet'.

Ref:

- https://docs.microsoft.com/en-us/microsoft-365/enterprise/connect-an-on-premises-network-to-a-microsoft-azure-virtual-network?view=o365-worldwide

Azure DevTest labs

47. Which of the following options isn't a benefit of ExpressRoute?

1. Redundant connectivity
1. Consistent network throughput
2. Encrypted network communication
3. Access to Microsoft cloud services

Correct Answer: 3

Explanation

DevTest Labs creates labs consisting of pre-configured bases or Azure Resource Manager templates. These have all the necessary tools and software that you can use to create environments. You can create environments in a few minutes, as opposed to hours or days.

Ref:

- https://docs.microsoft.com/en-us/azure/devtest-labs/devtest-lab-overview

48. Your company has a team of developers that plans to deploy 100 customized virtual machines each week and deallocated them after use. Half of the virtual machines will run Windows Server 2019 and the other half will run Windows Server 2016. You need to recommend which Azure service will minimize the administrative effort required to deploy and deallocate the virtual machines. What should you recommend?

1. Azure Reserved Virtual Machines (VM) Instances
1. Azure virtual machine scale sets
2. Azure DevTest Labs

3. Microsoft Managed Desktop

Correct Answer: 3

Explanation

By using DevTest Labs, you can test the latest versions of your applications by doing the following tasks:

- Quickly provision Windows and Linux environments by using reusable templates and artifacts.
- Easily integrate your deployment pipeline with DevTest Labs to provision on-demand environments.
- Scale up your load testing by provisioning multiple test agents and create pre-provisioned environments for training and demos.

Ref:

- https://azure.microsoft.com/en-us/services/devtest-lab/

Azure Machine Learning

49. Which of the following solutions should your company use to build, test, and deploy predictive analytics on an Artificial Intelligence (AI) solution deployed on Azure?

1. Azure Machine Learning studio
   1. Azure Cosmos DB
   2. Azure Logic Apps
   3. None of the above

Correct Answer: 1

Explanation

Machine Learning Studio is a powerfully simple browser-based, visual drag-and-drop authoring environment where no coding is necessary. Go from idea to deployment in a matter of clicks. Azure Machine Learning is designed for applied machine learning. Use best-in-class algorithms and a simple drag-and-drop interface-and go from idea to deployment in a matter of clicks.

Ref:

- https://docs.microsoft.com/en-us/learn/paths/build-ai-solutions-with-azure-ml-service/

Azure Cognitive Services

50. Which of the following listed Azure tools is a simplified tool to build artificial intelligence (AI) applications

1. Azure DevTest Labs
1. Azure IoT Hub
2. Azure Databricks
3. Azure Cognitive Services

Correct Answer: 4

Explanation

Cognitive Services brings AI within reach of every developer'without requiring machine-learning expertise. All it takes is an API call to embed the ability to see, hear, speak, search, understand, and accelerate decision-making into your apps.

Ref:

- https://azure.microsoft.com/en-us/services/cognitive-services/

PART 4

Describe core solutions and management tools on Azure

Azure Advisor

1. Which task can you perform by using Azure Advisor?

1. Integrate Active Directory and Azure Active Directory (Azure AD).
1. Estimate the costs of an Azure solution.
2. Confirm that Azure subscription security follows best practices
3. Evaluate which on-premises resources can be migrated to Azure.

Correct Answer: 2

Explanation

Estimate the costs of an Azure solution. >The Advisor dashboard displays personalized recommendations for all your subscriptions. You can apply filters to display recommendations for specific subscriptions and resource types. The recommendations are divided into five categories: Cost, security, performance, operational excellence and reliability.

Ref:

- https://docs.microsoft.com/en-us/azure/advisor/advisor-overview

Azure Log Analytics

2. Which Azure service should you use to collect events from multiple resources and assemble them in one location for easier display?

1. Azure Event Hubs
1. Azure Analysis Services
2. Azure Monitor
3. Azure Log Analytics

Correct Answer: 4

Explanation

Log Analytics is a web tool used to write and execute Azure Monitor log queries. Open it by selecting Logs in the Azure Monitor menu. It starts with a new blank query.

Ref:

- https://docs.microsoft.com/en-us/azure/azure-monitor/log-query/log-analytics-tutorial

Azure Resource Manager

3. What does Programmatic Deployment Blade on Azure do?

1. Enables program deployment without user input
1. Initiate deploying their resources in a programmatic manner
2. See history of all deployments on Azure
3. None of the above

Explanation

Subscription blade has a programmatic deployment option, which is to INITIATE a programmatic deployment using ARM templates, but not to see history of deployments. To vie the history of deployments you have to go activity logs.

Ref:

- https://docs.microsoft.com/en-us/azure/azure-resource-manager/templates/quickstart-create-templates-use-the-portal

4. Your company plans to migrate to Azure. The company has several departments. All the Azure resources used by each department will be managed by a department administrator. What are two possible techniques to segment Azure for the departments?

1. multiple subscriptions
1. multiple Azure Active Directory (Azure AD) directories
2. multiple regions
3. multiple resource groups

Correct Answer: 1

Explanation

if you have multiple departments then you would want to separate them into subscription and under subs you can add your multiple RGs. The answer should be A. If we create resource group for segmenting department, we will not be able to segment further for resource type, as resource group cannot be nested. This will create lots of issue for department admin So we need to segment by subscription and then the department admin can create resource group as per need.

Ref:

- https://docs.microsoft.com/en-us/azure/azure-resource-manager/management/tag-resources

Azure Resource Provider

5. Which of the following options is the main role of Azure Resource provider blade?

1. Configure resources usage
1. See history of deployments made in a resource group
2. Show resources that are registered to a specific subscription
3. Show all resources that are provided by Azure

Correct Answer: 3

Explanation

When deploying resources, you frequently need to retrieve information about the resource providers and types. For example, if you want to store keys and secrets, you work with the Microsoft.KeyVault resource provider. This resource provider offers a resource type called vaults for creating the key vault.

Ref:

- https://docs.microsoft.com/en-us/azure/azure-resource-manager/management/resource-providers-and-types

Azure Storage Explorer

6. Which Microsoft Azure tool/s can you use when you want to need to move blueprint files into Azure?

1. Use Azure Storage Explorer to copy the files.
1. Use the Azure Import/Export service.
2. Generate a shared access signature (SAS). Map a drive, and then copy the files by using File Explorer.
3. Generate an access key. Map a drive, and then copy the files by using File Explorer

Correct Answer: 1

Explanation

Use Azure Storage Explorer to copy the files.> Azure Storage Explorer is a free tool from Microsoft that allows you to work with Azure Storage data on Windows, macOS, and Linux. You can use it to upload and download data from Azure blob storage.

Ref:

- https://docs.microsoft.com/en-us/azure/vs-azure-tools-storage-manage-with-storage-explorer?tabs=windows

Azure Storage

7. You plan to use the Azure Import/Export service to copy files to a storage account. Which two files should you create before you prepare the drives for the import job?

1. A driveset CSV file.
1. B. A JSON configuration file.
2. C. A PowerShell PS1 file.
3. D. An XML manifest file.
4. E. A dataset CSV file.

Correct Answer: 1,5

Explanation

A driveset CSV file. Modify the driveset.csv file in the root folder where the tool resides.

A dataset CSV file. Modify the dataset.csv file in the root folder where the tool resides. Depending on whether you want to import a file or folder or both, add entries in the dataset.csv file.

Ref:

- https://docs.microsoft.com/en-us/azure/storage/common/storage-import-export-data-to-files?tabs=azure-portal

8. You create an Azure Storage account and plan to create a file share. Users need to map a drive to the file share from home computers that run Windows 10. Which outbound port should you open between the home computers and the file share?

1. 80

1. 443
2. 445
3. 3389

Correct Answer: 3

Explanation

Azure Files is Microsoft?s easy-to-use cloud file system. Azure file shares can be seamlessly used in Windows and Windows Server. Prerequisites:

- **Storage account name:** To mount an Azure file share, you will need the name of the storage account.

- **Storage account key:** To mount an Azure file share, you will need the primary (or secondary) storage key. SAS keys are not currently supported for mounting.

- **Ensure port 445 is open:** The SMB protocol requires TCP port 445 to be open; connections will fail if port 445 is blocked.

You can check to see if your firewall is blocking port 445 with the Test-NetConnection cmdlet.

Ref:

- https://docs.microsoft.com/en-us/azure/storage/files/storage-how-to-create-file-share?tabs=azure-portal

Virtual Machines

9. Which of the following changes to a running Virtual Machine will cause a downtime of service hosted on it?

1. Add the Puppet Agent extension.
1. Change the size to D8s v3.
2. Add a 500-GB managed disk.
3. Attach an additional network interface.

Correct Answer: 2

Explanation

You can resize when the VM is online. but it performs a restart in the backend. The physical hardware currently hosting your VM. If the physical hardware currently running your virtual machine also supports your desired new size, then it is very easy to change the VM size through a simple size change operation which results in a VM reboot.

Ref:

- https://azure.microsoft.com/en-us/blog/resize-virtual-machines/

10. Which blade on Azure portal should you use to monitor a Linux Virtual Machine that you have deployed on your subscription account?

1. The AzurePerformanceDiagnostics extension.
1. Azure HDInsight.
2. Linux Diagnostic Extension (LAD) 3.0.
3. Azure Analysis Services.

Correct Answer: 3

Explanation

The Linux Diagnostic Extension helps a user monitor the health of a Linux VM running on Microsoft Azure. Collects system performance metrics from the VM and stores them in a specific table in a designated storage account. Retrieves log events from syslog and stores them in a specific table in the designated storage account.

Ref:

- https://docs.microsoft.com/en-us/azure/virtual-machines/extensions/diagnostics-linux

11. Azure Performance Diagnostics VM Extension helps collect performance diagnostic data from Windows VMs. Which of the following listed Windows OS does not support Azure Performance diagnostics extension?

1. Windows Server 2008 R2
1. Windows Server 2012
2. Windows 7
3. Windows 8

Correct Answer: 3

Explanation

This extension can be installed on Windows Server 2019, Windows Server 2016, Windows Server 2012 R2, Windows Server 2012, Windows Server 2008 R2, Windows 10, Windows 8.1 and Windows 8

Ref:

- https://docs.microsoft.com/en-us/azure/virtual-machines/troubleshooting/performance-diagnostics-vm-extension#prerequisites

12. You have an Azure subscription regularly create and delete virtual machines used for testing purposes. You try to delete some VMs and unattached disks can't be deleted. What should you do to clear the unattached disks?

1. From Microsoft Azure Storage Explorer, view the Account Management properties.
1. From the Azure portal, configure the Advisor recommendations.
2. From Azure Cost Management, view Advisor Recommendations.
3. 'From Azure Cost Management, view Cost Analysis.

Correct Answer: 1

Explanation

You can find unused disks in the Azure Storage Explorer console. Once you drill down to the Blob containers under a storage account, you can see the lease state of the residing VHD (the lease state determines if the VHD is being used by any resource) and the VM to which it is leased out. If you find that the lease state and the VM fields are blank, it means that the VHD in question is unused. The screenshot below shows two active VHDs being used by VMs as data and OS disks. The name of the VM and lease state are shown in the "VM Name" and "Lease State" columns, respectively.

Referenc:

- https://docs.microsoft.com/en-us/azure/virtual-machines/windows/find-unattached-disks

13. You plan to back up an Azure virtual machine and discover that the Backup Pre-Check status displays a status of Warning. What is a possible cause of the Warning status?

1. VM is stopped.
1. 'VM does not have the latest version of WaAppAgent.exe installed.
2. VM has an unmanaged disk.
3. 'A Recovery Services vault is unavailable.

Correct Answer: 2

Explanation

The Warning state indicates one or more issues in VM's configuration that might lead to backup failures and provides recommended steps to ensure successful backups. Not having the latest VM Agent installed, for example, can cause backups to fail intermittently and falls in this class of issues.

Ref:

- https://azure.microsoft.com/en-us/blog/azure-vm-backup-pre-checks/

14. Which of the following costs does Azure continue charging you when you deallocate a Virtual Machine?

1. Connected Network Interface charge
1. The VM Size charges
2. The connected storage charge
3. Connected Network security group charge

Correct Answer: 3

Explanation

Connected storage charge > When an Azure virtual machine is stopped, you don?t pay for the virtual machine. However, you do still pay for the storage costs associated to the virtual machine. The most common storage costs are for the disks attached to the virtual machines. There are also other storage costs associated with a virtual machine such as storage for diagnostic data and virtual machine backups.

Ref:

- https://azure.microsoft.com/en-us/pricing/details/virtual-machines/

15. Which of the following code snippets on creating a Windows server 2019 Virtual Machine via Azure CLI named VM1 with username Abby. The VM must be created in resource group RGAbby?

1. az vm create --resource-group RG1 --name VM1 --image Windows2019 --Username-Abby
1. az vm create --resource-group RG1 --name VM1 --image Windows2019 --Username-RGAbby
2. az vm create --resource-group RGAbby --name VM1 --image Windows2019 --Username-Abby
3. az vm create --resource-group RGAbby --name Abby --image Windows2019 --Username-Abby

Explanation

az vm create --resource-group RGAbby --name VM1 --image Windows2019 --Username-Abby.

Reference:

- > https://docs.microsoft.com/en-us/azure/virtual-machines/windows/cli-ps-findimage

Backup policy

16. You have an Azure virtual machine protected by Azure Backup. You delete the VM and need to remove the backup data stored. What should you do first?

1. Delete the Recovery Services vault.
1. Delete the storage account.
2. Stop the backup.
3. Modify the backup policy

Correct Answer: 4

Explanation

With the release of backup policy management, customers can manage backup policies and model them to meet their changing requirements from a single window. Customers can edit a policy, associate more virtual machines to a policy, and delete unnecessary policies to meet their compliance requirements.

Ref:

- https://docs.microsoft.com/en-us/azure/virtual-machines/windows/find-unattached-disks

Azure Products Status

17. Azure services in public preview can be used in production environments.

1. Yes
1. No

Correct Answer: 1

Explanation

You can use services in public preview in production environments. However, you should be aware that the service may have faults, is not subject to an SLA and may be withdrawn without notice.

Ref:

- https://azure.microsoft.com/en-us/support/legal/preview-supplemental-terms/

Azure Pricing

18. Does Storing 1 TB data In Azure Blob storage will always cost the same, regardless of the Azure region in which the data less located.

1. TRUE
1. FALSE

Correct Answer: 2

Explanation

the price of Azure storage varies by region. If you use the Azure storage pricing page, you can select different regions and see how the price changes per region.

Ref:

- https://azure.microsoft.com/en-us/pricing/details/storage/

19. Transferring data between Azure storage accounts in different Azure regions is free.

1. TRUE
1. FALSE

Correct Answer: 2

Explanation

You would be charge for the read operations of the source storage account and write operations in the destination storage account.

Ref:

- https://azure.microsoft.com/en-us/pricing/details/bandwidth/

Azure Service Health

20. From which of the following blade can you view the health of all the services deployed to an Azure environment and all the other services available in Azure?

1. Azure Monitor
1. Azure Analysis Services
2. Azure HDInsights
3. Azure Service Health

Correct Answer: 4

Explanation

Azure Service Health notifies you about Azure service incidents and planned maintenance so you can take action to mitigate downtime. Configure customizable cloud alerts and use your personalized dashboard to analyse health issues, monitor the impact to your cloud resources, get guidance and support, and share details and updates.

Ref:

- https://azure.microsoft.com/en-us/features/service-health/

21. Which Azure blade can you use as an Azure Admin to create a rule to be alerted if an Azure service fails?

1. Azure HDInsight
1. Azure Service Health
2. Azure Monitor
3. Azure Analysis Services

Correct Answer: 2

Explanation

Azure Service Health notifies you about Azure service incidents and planned maintenance so you can take action to mitigate downtime. Configure customizable cloud alerts and use your personalized dashboard to analyse health issues, monitor the impact to your cloud resources, get guidance and support, and share details and updates.

Ref:

- https://azure.microsoft.com/en-us/features/service-health/

Cognitive services

22. Which of this is a simplified tool to build artificial intelligence (AI) applications

1. Azure DevTest Labs
1. Azure IoT Hub
2. Azure Databricks
3. Azure Cognitive Services

Correct Answer: 4

Explanation

> Cognitive Services brings AI within reach of every developer?without requiring machine-learning expertise. All it takes is an API call to embed the ability to see, hear, speak, search, understand, and accelerate decision-making into your apps.

Ref:

- https://azure.microsoft.com/en-us/services/cognitive-services/

Azure HDInisight

23. Choose the tool used as open-source framework for the distributed processing and analysis of big data sets in clusters in Azure.

1. Azure IoT Hub
1. Azure Databricks
2. Azure HDInisight
3. Azure Datalake Analytics

Correct Answer: 3

Explanation

> Easily run popular open-source frameworks?including Apache Hadoop, Spark, and Kafka?using Azure HDInsight, a cost-effective, enterprise-grade service for open-source analytics. Effortlessly process massive amounts of data and get all the benefits of the broad open-source ecosystem with the global scale of Azure.

Ref:

- https://azure.microsoft.com/en-us/services/hdinsight/

Container Instances

24. What does Azure Container instances do?

1. Provide Operating system virtualization
1. Provide portable environment for virtualized applications
2. Build and deploy virtualized environments to install applications
3. Provide platform for Serverless code.

Correct Answer: 2

Explanation

Azure Container Instances is a solution for any scenario that can operate in isolated containers, without orchestration. Run event-driven applications, quickly deploy from your container development pipelines, and run data processing and build jobs.

Ref:

- https://azure.microsoft.com/en-us/services/container-instances/#overview

Fault Tolerance

25. You have an on-premises network that contains several servers you plan to migrate Azure. You need to recommend a solution to ensure that some of the servers are available if a single Azure data center goes offline for an extended period. What should you include in the recommendation?

1. fault tolerance
1. elasticity
2. scalability
3. low latency

Correct Answer: 1

Explanation

Correct Answer: A. fault tolerance > In the event of a failure, the Azure infrastructure (the Fabric Controller) reacts immediately to restore services and infrastructure. For example, if a virtual machine (VM) fails due to a hardware failure on the physical host, the Fabric Controller moves that VM to another physical node based on the same hard disk stored in Azure storage. Azure is similarly capable of coordinating upgrades and updates in such a way as to avoid service downtime.

Ref:

- https://docs.microsoft.com/en-us/archive/msdn-magazine/2015/september/microsoft-azure-fault-tolerance-pitfalls-and-resolutions-in-the-cloud

Virtual Network

26. Your company plans to move several servers to Azure. The company?s compliance policy states that a server named Server1 must be on a separate network segment. You are evaluating which Azure services can be used to meet the compliance policy requirements. Which Azure solution should you recommend?

1. a resource group for Server1 and another resource group for all the other servers
1. a virtual network for Server1 and another virtual network for all the other servers
2. a VPN for Server1 and a virtual network gateway for each other server
3. one resource group for all the servers and a resource lock for Server1

Correct Answer: 2

Explanation

a virtual network for Server1 and another virtual network for all the other servers > Virtual networks are created within a subscription in private address spaces and provide network level containment of resources with no traffic allowed by default between any two virtual networks. Like subscriptions, any communication between virtual networks needs to be explicitly provisioned.

Ref:

- https://docs.microsoft.com/en-us/azure/architecture/reference-architectures/hybrid-networking/network-level-segmentation

Logic apps

27. Your company have an on-premises application that sends email notifications automatically based on a rule to customers every end of the week or when an event happens. You plan to migrate the application to Azure and need to recommend a serverless computing solution for the application.

1. a web app
1. a server image in Azure Marketplace
2. a logic app
3. an API app

Correct Answer: 3

Explanation

Azure Logic Apps is a cloud service that helps you schedule, automate, and orchestrate tasks, business processes, and workflows when you need to integrate apps, data, systems, and services across enterprises or organizations. ... Move uploaded files from an SFTP or FTP server to Azure Storage.

Ref:

- https://docs.microsoft.com/en-us/azure/logic-apps/

Availability Zones

28. An Availability Zone in Azure has physically separate locations_____ ?

1. within a single country
1. within a single Azure region
2. within multiple Azure regions
3. within a single Azure datacenter

Correct Answer: 2

Explanation

All Azure management services are architected to be resilient from region-level failures. In the spectrum of failures, one or more Availability Zone failures within a region have a smaller failure radius compared to an entire region failure. Azure can recover from a zone-level failure of management services within a region.

Ref:

- https://docs.microsoft.com/en-us/azure/availability-zones/az-region

Azure regions

29. Who can use the services of Azure United Kingdom (UK)?

1. Only the residents of Britain
1. Only the residents of the larger United Kingdom
2. Only the residents of European Union
3. Any Azure user that requires their data to reside in UK

Correct Answer: 4

Explanation

All Azure regions are open to anyone or any company that choose to have their resources hosted there excluding Azure Governance regions.

Ref:

- https://azure.microsoft.com/en-au/global-infrastructure/geographies/

Azure Firewall

30. Which service provides network traffic filtering across multiple Azure subscriptions and virtual networks?

1. Azure Firewall
1. an application security group
2. Azure DDoS protection
3. a network security group (NSG)

Correct Answer: 1

Explanation

Azure Firewall is a fully stateful, centralized network firewall as-a-service, which provides network- and application-level protection across different subscriptions and virtual networks.

Ref:

- https://docs.microsoft.com/en-us/azure/firewall/firewall-faq#:~:text=Azure%20Firewall%20is%20a%20fully,different%20subscriptions%20and%20virtual%20networks

Azure Key Vault

31. Which of the following Azure service should you use to store certificates?

1. Azure Security Center
1. an Azure Storage account
2. Azure Key Vault
3. Azure Information Protection

Correct Answer: 3

Explanation

Azure Key Vault is a secure store for storage various types of sensitive information including passwords and certificates. Azure Key Vault can be used to Securely store and tightly control access to tokens, passwords, certificates, API keys, and other secrets. Secrets and keys are safeguarded by Azure, using industry-standard algorithms, key lengths, and hardware security modules (HSMs). The HSMs used are Federal Information Processing Standards (FIPS) 140-2 Level 2 validated. Access to a key vault requires proper authentication and authorization before a caller (user or application) can get access. Authentication establishes the identity of the caller, while authorization determines the operations that they are allowed to perform.

Ref:

- https://docs.microsoft.com/en-us/azure/key-vault/

Azure Monitor

32. From which Azure blade given below can you can view which user turned off a specific virtual machine during the last 30 days?

1. Azure Monitor
1. Azure Event Hubs
2. Azure Activity Log
3. Azure Service Health

Correct Answer: 3

Explanation

You would use the Azure Activity Log, not Azure Monitor to view which user turned off a specific virtual machine during the last 30 days. Activity logs are kept for 90 days. You can query for any range of dates, as long as the starting date isn?t more than 90 days in the past

Ref:

- https://docs.microsoft.com/en-us/azure/azure-monitor/platform/activity-log#:~:text=The%20Activity%20log%20is%20a,entries%2 0with%20PowerShell%20and%20CLI

33. Which of the following monitoring services is a platform for collecting, analyzing, visualizing, and potentially taking action based on the metric and logging data from your entire Azure and on-premises environment?

1. Azure Advisor
1. Azure Analytics services
2. Azure Monitor

3. Azure HDInsight

Correct Answer: 3

Explanation

Azure Monitor helps you maximize the availability and performance of your applications and services. It delivers a comprehensive solution for collecting, analyzing, and acting on telemetry from your cloud and on-premises environments.

Ref:

- https://docs.microsoft.com/en-us/azure/azure-monitor/overview#:~:text=Azure%20Monitor%20helps%20you%20maximize,cloud%20and%20on%2Dpremises%20environments.&text=Collect%20data%20from%20monitored%20resources%20using%20Azure%20Monitor%20Metrics

Azure Database

34. Which two of the following tools can be used to transfer on-premise Database to Azure?

1. Azure SQL Managed Instance
1. Azure Database migration service
2. Azure Data Lake
3. Native backup and restore
4. Azure MariaDB

Correct Answer: 4,5

Explanation

Azure SQL Managed Instance makes it easy to migrate your on-premises data on SQL Server to the cloud using the Azure Database Migration Service (DMS) or native backup and restore. After you have discovered all of the features that your company uses, you need to assess which on-premises SQL Server instances you can migrate to Azure SQL Managed Instance to see if you have any blocking issues. Once you have resolved any issues, you can migrate your data, then cutover from your on-premises SQL Server to your Azure SQL Managed Instance by changing the connection string in your applications.

Ref:

- https://docs.microsoft.com/en-us/learn/modules/azure-database-fundamentals/azure-sql-managed-instance

35. Azure Database for MySQL is a relational database service in the cloud, and it's based on the MySQL Community Edition database engine. Azure DB for MYSQL delivers the following except?

1. Scale as needed, within seconds.
1. Ability to protect sensitive data at-rest and in-motion.

2. ' Automatic backups.

3. Automatic Load Balancing

Correct Answer: 4

Explanation

Azure Database for MySQL delivers:

- Built-in high availability with no additional cost.
- Predictable performance and inclusive, pay-as-you-go pricing.
- Scale as needed, within seconds.
- Ability to protect sensitive data at-rest and in-motion.
- Automatic backups.
- Enterprise-grade security and compliance.

These capabilities require almost no administration, and all are provided at no additional cost.

Ref:

- https://docs.microsoft.com/en-us/learn/modules/azure-database-fundamentals/azure-mysql-database

36. Your development team is interested in writing Graph-based applications that take advantage of the Gremlin API. Which option would be ideal for that scenario?

1. Azure Cosmos DB
1. Azure Databricks
2. Azure Database for PostgreSQL
3. Azure SQL Database

Correct Answer: 1

Explanation

Azure Cosmos DB supports SQL, MongoDB, Cassandra, Tables, and Gremlin APIs. Azure Cosmos DB supports schema-less data, which lets you build highly responsive and "Always On" applications to support constantly changing data. You can use this feature to store data that's updated and maintained by users around the world

Ref:

- https://docs.microsoft.com/en-us/learn/modules/azure-database-fundamentals/azure-cosmos-db

Azure Synapse Analytics

37. You work for a company that has millions of log entries that it wants to analyze. Which option would be ideal for analysis?

1. Azure Cosmos DB
1. Azure SQL Database
2. Azure Database for PostgreSQL
3. Azure Synapse Analytics

Correct Answer: 4

Explanation

Azure Synapse Analytics is a limitless analytics service that brings together enterprise data warehousing and big data analytics. You can query data on your terms by using either serverless or provisioned resources at scale. You have a unified experience to ingest, prepare, manage, and serve data for immediate BI and machine learning needs.

Ref:

- https://docs.microsoft.com/en-us/learn/modules/azure-database-fundamentals/azure-big-data-analytics

Azure Batch

38. Azure Batch enables large-scale parallel and high-performance computing (HPC) batch jobs with the ability to scale to tens, hundreds, or thousands of VMs. Which of the following tasks is not performed by an Azure batch?

1. Starts a pool of compute VMs for you.
1. '' Installs applications and staging data.
2. ' Runs jobs with as many tasks as you have.
3. Request VPN connection with on-premises network from the Virtual Network in Azure.
4. '' Identifies failures

Correct Answer: 4

Explanation

Azure Batch can perform all those tasks except establish a connection outside the VMs or the Virtual Networks unless directed to by the administrator.

Ref:

- https://docs.microsoft.com/en-us/learn/modules/azure-compute-fundamentals/azure-virtual-machines

Kubernetes service

39. Azure Container instances offers the fastest and simplest way to run a container in Azure without having to manage any virtual machines or adopt any additional services. What is the name given to Azure services where you need run multiple Container Instances?

1. Azure Data Lake
1. Azure Microservice instances
2. Azure Kubernetes
3. Azure Cosmos Instances

Correct Answer: 3

Explanation

The task of automating, managing, and interacting with a large number of containers is known as orchestration. Azure Kubernetes Service is a complete orchestration service for containers with distributed architectures and large volumes of containers. Orchestration is the task of automating and managing a large number of containers and how they interact.

Ref:

- https://azure.microsoft.com/services/kubernetes-service

Azure app services

40. Which of the following are types of App services that can be hosted on Azure?

1. API apps
1. Node Js
2. WebJobs
3. React Js
4. Mobile apps

Correct Answer: 1,3,5

Explanation

With App Service, you can host most common app service styles like: Web apps, API apps, WebJobs, Mobile apps. App Service handles most of the infrastructure decisions you deal with in hosting web-accessible apps. Node and React Js are both frameworks fo building Apps.

Ref:

- https://docs.microsoft.com/en-us/learn/modules/azure-compute-fundamentals/azure-app-services

Azure Functions

41. Azure Functions can run locally or in the cloud while Azure Logic apps can only run in the cloud. Is this statement correct?

1. TRUE
1. FALSE

Correct Answer: 1

Explanation

With Functions, you write code to complete each step and hence can run both locally and online but with Logic Apps, you use a GUI to define the actions and how they relate to one another which is only hosted in Azure.

Ref:

- https://docs.microsoft.com/en-us/learn/modules/azure-compute-fundamentals/azure-functions

42. Which of the following services should be used when the primary concern is to perform work in response to an event (often via a REST command) that needs a response in a few seconds?

1. Azure Functions
1. Azure App Service
2. Azure Container Instances

Correct Answer: 1

Explanation

Azure Functions is used when you need to perform work in response to an event (often via a REST request), timer, or message from another Azure service, and when that work can be completed quickly, within seconds or less.

Ref:

- https://docs.microsoft.com/en-us/azure/azure-functions/functions-create-serverless-api

Windows Virtual Desktop

43. What do we call desktop and application virtualization service that runs on the cloud and enables your users to use a cloud-hosted version of Windows from any location and from any computer device?

1. Azure Virtual Machine
1. Azure Kubernetes
2. Windows Virtual Desktop
3. Windows Cloud share

Correct Answer: 3

Explanation

Windows Virtual Desktop on Azure is a desktop and application virtualization service that runs on the cloud. It enables your users to use a cloud-hosted version of Windows from any location. Windows Virtual Desktop works across devices like Windows, Mac, iOS, Android, and Linux. It works with apps that you can use to access remote desktops and apps. You can also use most modern browsers to access Windows Virtual Desktop-hosted experience.

Ref:

- https://docs.microsoft.com/en-us/learn/modules/azure-compute-fundamentals/windows-virtual-desktop

44. Your company has a team of remote workers that need to use Windows-based software to develop your company's applications, but your team members are using various operating systems like MacOS, Linux, and Windows. Which Azure compute service would help resolve this scenario?

1. Azure App Service

1. Windows Virtual Desktop
2. Azure Container Instances

Correct Answer: 2

Explanation

Windows Virtual Desktop enables your team members to run Windows in the cloud, with access to the required applications for your company's needs

Ref:

- https://docs.microsoft.com/en-us/learn/modules/azure-compute-fundamentals/windows-virtual-desktop

Virtual Machines Scale sets

45. Which Azure compute resource can be deployed to manage a set of identical virtual machines?

1. Virtual machine availability sets
1. Virtual machine availability zones
2. Virtual machine scale sets
3. Virtual Networks Interface

Correct Answer: 3

Explanation

Virtual machine scale sets let you deploy and manage a set of identical virtual machines. Azure virtual machine scale sets let you create and manage a group of load balanced VMs. The number of VM instances can automatically increase or decrease in response to demand or a defined schedule

Ref:

- https://docs.microsoft.com/en-us/azure/virtual-machine-scale-sets/overview#:~:text=Azure%20virtual%20machine%20scale%20sets%20let%20you%20create%20and%20manage, demand%20or%20a%20defined%20schedule

Azure Machine Learning

46. You need to predict future behaviours based on previous actions. Which product option should you select as a candidate?

1. Azure Machine Learning
1. Azure Bot Service
2. Azure Cognitive Services

Correct Answer: 1

Explanation

Azure Machine Learning enables you to build models to predict the likelihood of a future result. It should not be eliminated as a candidate.

Azure Bot Service

47. You need to create a human-computer interface that uses natural language to answer customer questions. Which product option should you select as a candidate?

1. Azure Machine Learning
1. Azure Cognitive Services
2. Azure Bot Service

Correct Answer: 3

Explanation

Azure Bot Service creates virtual agent solutions that utilize natural language. It should not be eliminated as a candidate.

Ref:

- https://azure.microsoft.com/en-us/services/bot-services/

Azure cognitive Service

48. You need to identify the content of product images to automatically create alt tags for images formatted properly. Which product option is the best candidate?

1. Azure Machine Learning
1. Azure Cognitive Services
2. Azure Bot Service
3. Azure IoT Hub

Correct Answer: 2

Explanation

Azure Cognitive Services includes Vision services that can identify the content of an image. Azure Cognitive Services is the best candidate. Cognitive Services brings AI within reach of every developer?without requiring machine-learning expertise. All it takes is an API call to embed the ability to see, hear, speak, search, understand, and accelerate decision-making into your apps

Ref:

- https://azure.microsoft.com/en-us/services/cognitive-services/

Azure DevOps

49. which of the following is an automated test tool that can be used in a CI/CD pipeline to ensure quality before a software release.

1. Azure Pipelines
1. Azure Repos
2. Azure Board
3. Azure Test Plans

Correct Answer: 4

Explanation

Azure Test plans provides a browser-based test management solution for exploratory, planned manual, and user acceptance testing. Azure Test Plans also provides a browser extension for exploratory testing and gathering feedback from stakeholders.

Ref:

- https://azure.microsoft.com/en-us/services/devops/test-plans/

50. Which of the following Azure solutions does not fall under the wide DevOps solutions?

1. Azure Board
1. Azure Test Plans
2. Azure DevTest Labs
3. Azure Pipelines
4. Azure Repos

Correct Answer: 3

Explanation

> Azure DevTest Labs is an independent solution from the DevOps solution. DevOps solutions are made of : Azure Board, Azure Test Plans, Azure Pipelines, Azure Repos and Azure Artifacts

Ref:

- https://docs.microsoft.com/en-us/learn/modules/azure-devops-devtest-labs/2-identify-product-options

51. Which service lacks features to assign individual developers? tasks to work on?

1. Azure Board
1. Azure Test Plans
2. Azure DevTest Labs
3. Azure Pipelines

Correct Answer: 4

Explanation

Azure Pipelines is a CI/CD tool for building an automated toolchain. It lacks features to assign tasks for individual developers to work on. However, it can automate other tools to assign tasks to users.

Ref:

- https://docs.microsoft.com/en-us/azure/devops/pipelines/?view=azure-devops

52. Which service could help you manage the VMs that your developers and testers need to ensure that your new app works across various operating systems?

1. Azure DevTest Labs
1. Azure Test Labs
2. Azure Repos

Correct Answer: 1

Explanation

Azure DevTest Labs is used to manage VMs for testing, including configuration, provisioning, and automatic de-provisioning.

Ref:

- https://docs.microsoft.com/en-us/learn/modules/azure-devops-devtest-labs/2-identify-product-options

Azure Advisor

53. Which of the following monitoring services evaluates your Azure resources and makes recommendations to help improve reliability, security, and performance, achieve operational excellence, and reduce costs?

1. Azure Monitor
1. Azure Advisor
2. Azure HDInsight
3. Azure Analytics services

Correct Answer: 2

Explanation

Azure Advisor evaluates your Azure resources and makes recommendations to help improve reliability, security, and performance, achieve operational excellence, and reduce costs. Advisor is designed to help you save time on cloud optimization. The recommendation service includes suggested actions you can take right away, postpone, or dismiss.

Ref:

- https://docs.microsoft.com/en-us/learn/modules/monitoring-fundamentals/2-identify-product-options2

Azure Portal

54. You're a developer new to Azure who needs to set up your first VM to host a process that runs nightly. Which of the following tools is your best choice?

1. ARM templates
1. Azure PowerShell
2. The Azure portal
3. The Azure CLI

Correct Answer: 3

Explanation

The Azure portal is a great place for newcomers to learn about Azure and set up their first resources and assign policies to the resources much more esily.

PART 5

Describe general security and network security features

Azure Security Center

1. Which of the following resources acts as a monitoring service that provides visibility of your security posture across all of your services, both on Azure and on-premises?

1. Azure Monitor
1. Azure Security Center
2. Azure Key Vault
3. Azure Information Protection

Correct Answer: 2

Explanation

Azure Security Center is a monitoring service that provides visibility of your security posture across all of your services, both on Azure and on-premises. The term security posture refers to cybersecurity policies and controls, as well as how well you can predict, prevent, and respond to security threats.

Ref:

- https://docs.microsoft.com/en-us/learn/modules/protect-against-security-threats-azure/2-protect-threats-security-center

2. What is Azure Security score?

1. Automatic application of the required security protocol in Azure.
1. Security recommendations number on azure resources.
2. 'measurement of an organization's security posture.
3. measurement of Azure resources security posture.

Correct Answer: 3

Explanation

Secure score is based on security controls, or groups of related security recommendations. Your score is based on the percentage of security controls that you satisfy. The more security controls you satisfy, the higher the score you receive. Your score improves when you remediate all of the recommendations for a single resource within a control.

Ref:

- https://docs.microsoft.com/en-us/azure/security-center/secure-score-security-controls/

3. Your company plans on having only certain applications run on its Azure Virtual Machines. Which of the following could help enforce that?

1. Connect your VMs to Azure Sentinel.
1. Create an application control rule in Azure Security Center.
2. Periodically run a script that lists the running processes on each VM. The IT manager can then shut down any applications that shouldn't be running.

Correct Answer: 2

Explanation

With Azure Security Center, you can define a list of allowed applications to ensure that only applications you allow can run. Azure Security Center can also detect and block malware from being installed on your VMs.

Ref:

- https://azure.microsoft.com/en-us/services/security-center/

4. Azure Monitor autoscale provide a common set of autoscaling functionality for virtual machine scale sets, Azure App Service, and Azure Cloud Service. Scaling can be performed on a schedule, or based on a runtime metric, such as CPU or memory usage.

Ref:

- https://docs.microsoft.com/en-us/azure/azure-monitor/platform/autoscale-overview

1. TRUE
1. FALSE

Correct Answer: 1

Explanation

Azure Security Center is a unified infrastructure security management system that strengthens the security posture of your data centers, and provides advanced threat protection across your hybrid workloads in the cloud ? whether they?re in Azure or not ? as well as on premises.

Ref:

- https://azure.microsoft.com/en-us/blog/azure-security-center-extends-advanced-threat-protection-to-hybrid-cloud-workloads/

5. Which of the following Azure Security Center features are usually provided free?

1. File Integrity monitoring
1. Continuous Assessment
2. Azure Score
3. Adaptive applications control
4. Native Vulnerability assessment

Correct Answer: 2,3

Explanation

Continuous assessment and security recommendations, and Azure secure score, are free in Azure Security center. The rest of features are charged differently.

Ref:

- https://docs.microsoft.com/en-us/azure/security-center/security-center-pricing

6. From which azure Blade can you download a Regulatory Compliance report?

1. Azure Service Health
1. Azure Monitor
2. Azure Security Center
3. Azure Advisor

Correct Answer: 3

Explanation

The advanced monitoring capabilities in Security Center also let you track and manage compliance and governance over time. The overall compliance provides you with a measure of how much your subscriptions are compliant with policies associated with your workload.

Ref:

- https://docs.microsoft.com/en-us/azure/security-center/security-center-compliance-dashboard

Azure Sentinel

7. Azure Sentinel is Microsoft's cloud-based SIEM system. It uses intelligent security analytics and threat analysis. Which of the following is NOT a task performed by Azure Sentinel?

1. Collect cloud data at scale
1. Detect previously undetected threats
2. Delete available threats automatically
3. Investigate threats with artificial intelligence

Correct Answer: 3

Explanation

Azure Sentinel enables you to:

- **Collect cloud data at scale:** Collect data across all users, devices, applications, and infrastructure, both on-premises and from multiple clouds.
- **Detect previously undetected threats:** Minimize false positives by using Microsoft's comprehensive analytics and threat intelligence.
- **Investigate threats with artificial intelligence:** Examine suspicious activities at scale, tapping into years of cybersecurity experience from Microsoft.
- **Respond to incidents rapidly:** Utilize built-in orchestration and automation of common tasks.

8. What's the easiest way for your company to combine security data from all of its monitoring tools in Azure into a single report that it can take action on?

1. Collect security data in Azure Sentinel.
1. Build a custom tool that collects security data and displays a report through a web application

2. Look through each security log daily and email a summary to your team.

Correct Answer: 1

Explanation

Azure Sentinel is Microsoft's cloud-based SIEM. A SIEM aggregates security data from many different sources to provide additional capabilities for threat detection and responding to threats.

Ref:

- https://docs.microsoft.com/en-us/azure/sentinel/

Azure key vault

9. Azure Key Vault is used to store secrets for?

1. Azure Active Directory (Azure AD) user accounts
1. Azure Active Directory (Azure AD) administrative accounts
2. Personally Identifiable Information (PII)
3. Server applications

Correct Answer: 1

Explanation

Azure Key Vault is a centralized cloud service for storing your application secrets. Key Vault helps you control your applications' secrets by keeping them in a single, central location and by providing secure access, permissions control, and access logging capabilities.

Ref:

- https://docs.microsoft.com/en-us/azure/key-vault/key-vault-overview

10. Your company plans to automate the deployment of servers to Azure. Your manager is concerned that you may expose administrative credentials during the deployment. Which Azure solution that encrypts the administrative credentials during the deployment should you use?

1. Azure Key Vault
1. Azure Information Protection
2. Azure Security Center
3. Azure Multi-Factor Authentication (MFA)

Correct Answer: 1

Azure Key Vault is a centralized cloud service for storing your application secrets. Key Vault helps you control your applications' secrets by keeping them in a single, central location and by providing secure access, permissions control, and access logging capabilities.

Ref:

- https://docs.microsoft.com/en-us/azure/key-vault/key-vault-overview

11. Which of the following are some of the benefits of Azure key Vault?

1. Secure stored keys and secrets
1. Retrieve security tokens
2. Encrypt documents and email messages
3. Monitor and report security threats in Azure AD
4. Simplified administration of application secrets

Correct Answer: 1,5

Explanation

The benefits of using Key Vault include:

- Centralized application secrets
- Securely stored secrets and keys
- Access monitoring and access control
- Simplified administration of application secrets
- Integration with other Azure services

Ref:

- https://docs.microsoft.com/en-us/learn/modules/protect-against-security-threats-azure/4-manage-secrets-key-vault

12. Which Azure service should you use to store certificates?

1. Azure Security Center
1. an Azure Storage account
2. Azure Key Vault
3. Azure Information Protection

Correct Answer: 3

Explanation

Azure Key Vault is a secure store for storage various types of sensitive information including passwords and certificates. Azure Key Vault can be used to Securely store and tightly control access to tokens, passwords, certificates, API keys, and other secrets. Secrets and keys are safeguarded by Azure, using industry-standard algorithms, key lengths, and hardware security modules (HSMs). The HSMs used are Federal Information Processing Standards (FIPS) 140-2 Level 2 validated. Access to a key vault requires proper authentication and authorization before a caller (user or application) can get access. Authentication establishes the identity of the caller, while authorization determines the operations that they are allowed to perform.

Ref:

- https://docs.microsoft.com/en-us/azure/key-vault/

Azure Active Directory

13. To what should an application connect to retrieve security tokens?

1. An Azure Storage account
1. Azure Active Directory (Azure AD)
2. Azure Key Vault
3. A certificate store

Correct Answer: 2

Explanation

Question is about accessing / retrieving security tokens token from Application & not storing the same. Azure Key Vault just stores the tokens and cannot be used to retrieve them. Microsoft identity platform authenticates users and provides security tokens, such as access token, refresh token, and ID token, that allow a client application to access protected resources on a resource server.

Ref:

- https://docs.microsoft.com/en-us/azure/active-directory/develop/security-tokens

14. Your on-premises network contains an Active Directory forest. With 1,000 user accounts. Your company plans to migrate all network resources to Azure and to decommission the on-premises data center. Recommend a solution to minimize the impact on users after the planned migration.

1. Implement Azure Multi-Factor Authentication (MFA)
1. Sync all the Active Directory user accounts to Azure Active Directory (Azure AD)
2. Instruct all users to change their password

3. Create a guest user account in Azure Active Directory (Azure AD) for each user

Correct Answer: 2

Explanation

Sync all the Active Directory user accounts to Azure Active Directory (Azure AD) > The easy way to do this is to sync all the Active Directory user accounts to Azure Active Directory (Azure AD). You can even sync their passwords to further minimize the impact on users. The tool you would use to sync the accounts is Azure AD Connect. The Azure Active Directory Connect synchronization services (Azure AD Connect sync) is a main component of Azure AD Connect. It takes care of all the operations that are related to synchronize identity data between your on-premises environment and Azure AD.

Ref:

- https://docs.microsoft.com/en-us/azure/active-directory/hybrid/how-to-connect-sync-whatis

Azure Information Protection

15. What can Azure Information Protection encrypt?

1. network traffic
1. documents and email messages
2. an Azure Storage account
3. an Azure SQL database

Correct Answer: 2

Explanation

documents and email messages. Azure Information Protection can encrypt documents and emails. Azure Information Protection is a cloud-based solution that helps an organization to classify and optionally, protect its documents and emails by applying labels. Labels can be applied automatically by administrators who define rules and conditions, manually by users, or a combination where users are given recommendations.

Ref:

- https://docs.microsoft.com/en-us/azure/information-protection/what-is-information-protection

16. What can Azure Information Protection encrypt?

1. network traffic
1. documents and email messages
2. an Azure Storage account
3. an Azure SQL database

Correct Answer: 2

Explanation

documents and email messages. Azure Information Protection is a cloud-based solution that helps an organization to classify and optionally, protect its documents and emails by applying labels. Labels can be applied automatically by administrators who define rules and conditions, manually by users, or a combination where users are given recommendations. The protection technology uses Azure Rights Management (often abbreviated to Azure RMS).

Ref:

- https://docs.microsoft.com/en-us/azure/information-protection/what-is-information-protection

Azure lifecycle

17. If Microsoft plans to end support for an Azure service that does NOT have a successor service, Microsoft will provide notification at least many months before?

1. 3
1. 12
2. 24
3. 6

Correct Answer: 2

Explanation

> For products governed by the Modern Lifecycle Policy, Microsoft will provide a minimum of 12 months' notification prior to ending support if no successor product or service is offered?excluding free services or preview releases.

Ref:

- https://docs.microsoft.com/en-us/lifecycle/policies/modern\

Cost management

18. What Azure service sends email alerts when the cost of the current billing period for an Azure subscription exceeds a specified limit?

1. Azure Advisor
1. Access control (IAM)
2. Budget alerts
3. Compliance

Correct Answer: 3

Explanation

Budget alerts notify you when spending, based on usage or cost, reaches or exceeds the amount defined in the alert condition of the budget. Cost Management budgets are created using the Azure portal or the Azure Consumption API.

Ref:

- Https://docs.microsoft.com/en-us/azure/cost-management-billing/costs/cost-mgt-alerts-monitor-usage-spending

Network Security Group

19. You have created a Virtual Machine in Azure. Now, you need to allow outside connect to the VM via TCP Port 8080. Which of the following listed service should you use to modify the target port?

1. Azure Firewall
1. Network Security Group
2. Azure Policies
3. Azure Web Firewall

Correct Answer: 2

Explanation

NSG default security rule denies access to TCP port 8080 by default and to use the port you have to change the inbound rules of the NSG connected to the VM. A network security group contains security rules that allow or deny inbound network traffic to, or outbound network traffic from, several types of Azure resources.

REF:

- https://docs.microsoft.com/en-us/azure/virtual-network/network-security-groups-overview

20. You plan to deploy several Azure virtual machines to be used by developer for pipeline App testing. You need to control the ports that devices on the Internet can use to access the virtual machines to prevent unauthorised access. What should you use?

1. a network security group (NSG)
1. an Azure Active Directory (Azure AD) role
2. an Azure Active Directory group
3. an Azure key vault

Correct Answer: 1

Explanation

You can use an Azure network security group to filter network traffic to and from Azure resources in an Azure virtual network. A network security group contains security rules that allow or deny inbound network traffic to, or outbound network traffic from, several types of Azure resources. For each rule, you can specify source and destination, port, and protocol.

Ref:

- https://docs.microsoft.com/en-us/azure/virtual-network/network-security-groups-overview

21. Your company plans to deploy several web servers and several database servers to Azure. You need to recommend an Azure solution to limit the types of connections from the web servers to the database servers. What should you include in the recommendation?

1. A route filter
1. Azure Bus Service
2. Local Network Gateway
3. Network Security Group

Correct Answer: 4

Explanation

You can filter network traffic to and from Azure resources in an Azure virtual network with a network security group. A network security group contains security rules that allow or deny inbound network traffic to, or outbound network traffic from, several types of Azure resources. To learn about which Azure resources can be deployed into a virtual network and have network security groups associated to them, see Virtual network integration for Azure services. For each rule, you can specify source and destination, port, and protocol.

Ref:

- https://docs.microsoft.com/en-us/azure/virtual-network/network-security-groups-overview

22. How can an organization most easily implement a deny by default policy so that VMs can't connect to each other?

1. Allocate each VM on its own virtual network.
1. Create a network security group rule that prevents access from another VM on the same network.
2. Configure Azure DDoS Protection to limit network access within the virtual network.

Correct Answer: 2

Explanation

A network security group rule enables you to filter traffic to and from resources by source and destination IP address, port, and protocol. Security rules in network security groups enable you to filter the type of network traffic that can flow in and out of virtual network subnets and network interfaces.

Ref:

- https://docs.microsoft.com/en-us/azure/virtual-network/manage-network-security-group

23. Your company has an Azure infrastructure deployed. Three virtual machines (VMs) are deployed to Azure as a three-tiered architecture. All three VMs host different items, with one hosting a front-end web application, one hosting a Microsoft SQL Server database and one hosting a business application programming interface (API). For public access, only the front-end web application be available and should be accessible over HTTP on port 80. All three VMs must be accessible over Remote Desktop Protocol (RDP) on port 222. There should be only one account able to access the VMs via RDP, and it should be yours. Can you determine how Network Security Groups (NSGs) will be used in this scenario? Identify the two ways NSG rules can be used below choices.

1. To ensure that only your account can use RDP to access the VMs
1. To ensure that only the front-end VM is publicly accessible over port 80
2. To ensure that all three VMs are accessible over port 222
3. Reviewed by executive management before being released to the public

Correct Answer: 2,3

Explanation

A Network Security Group (NSG) contains a list of security rules that allow or deny inbound or outbound network traffic based on source or destination IP address, port, and protocol. Under the Resource Manager deployment model, NSGs can be associated to subnets or individual network interfaces.

Ref:

- https://docs.microsoft.com/en-us/azure/site-recovery/concepts-network-security-group-with-site-recovery#:~:text=A%20Network%20Security%20Group%20(NSG,subnets%20or%20individual%20network%20interfaces

VM Dedicated Host

24. Which of the following Azure Services provides dedicated physical servers to host your Azure VMs for Windows and Linux isolated from workloads that other Azure customers?

1. Windows Virtual Desktop
1. Azure Virtual Machine
2. Azure Dedicated Host
3. Azure Containers

Correct Answer: 3

Explanation

On Azure, virtual machines (VMs) run on shared hardware that Microsoft manages. Although the underlying hardware is shared, your VM workloads are isolated from workloads that other Azure customers run.

Some organizations must follow regulatory compliance that requires them to be the only customer using the physical machine that hosts their virtual machines. Azure Dedicated Host provides dedicated physical servers to host your Azure VMs for Windows and Linux.

Ref:

- https://docs.microsoft.com/en-us/learn/modules/protect-against-security-threats-azure/6-host-virtual-machines-dedicated-hosts

Azure Firewall

25. What Azure service can you use to restrict the level of incoming traffic in an Azure environment made up of several Virtual Networks and Virtual Machines? Use several Virtual Network Gateways

1. Use several Expressroute circuits
1. Use one Network Security Group
2. Use one Azure Firewall

Correct Answer: 3

Explanation

Using a single Azure Firewall, you can centrally create, enforce, and log application and network connectivity policies across subscriptions and virtual networks. Azure Firewall uses a static public IP address for your virtual network resources allowing outside firewalls to identify traffic originating from your virtual network. The service is fully integrated with Azure Monitor for logging and analytics.

Ref:

- https://docs.microsoft.com/en-us/azure/firewall/overview

26. What is/are some of the features of Azure Firewall from the options listed below?

1. Inbound Destination Network Address Translation (DNAT) support
1. Block and edit ports in Virtual machine
2. Inbound and outbound filtering rules.
3. Provide security insights
4. Monitor incoming network for DDoS attacks

Correct Answer: 1,3

Explanation

Azure Firewall provides many features, including:

- Built-in high availability.

- Unrestricted cloud scalability.

- Inbound and outbound filtering rules.

- Inbound Destination Network Address Translation (DNAT) support.

- Azure Monitor logging.

You typically deploy Azure Firewall on a central virtual network to control general network access.

Ref:

- https://docs.microsoft.com/en-us/azure/firewall/

27. What's the best way for your company to limit all outbound traffic from VMs to known hosts?

1. Configure Azure DDoS Protection to limit network access to trusted ports and hosts.
1. Create application rules in Azure Firewall.
2. Ensure that all running applications communicate with only trusted ports and hosts.

Correct Answer: 2

Explanation

Azure Firewall enables you to limit outbound HTTP/S traffic to a specified list of fully qualified domain names (FQDNs). You can create security rules that performs exactly task you need on Azure Firewall.

Ref:

- https://cloudacademy.com/course/implementing-azure-network-security/creating-and-configuring-microsoft-azure-firewall/

28. Your company has deployed Azure. There are two subnets and you are required to filter traffic between them. Filtering should be based on three things: TCP/IP Protocol in use Source IP/address and port number Destination IP address and port number Solution. Which of the following would you suggest as a solution?

1. Azure Firewall to be deployed and configured as the traffic filter.
1. B' Deploy a VPN from Azure to on-premises network
2. ' Add a Network security group without any filters
3. Map Source Ip address and port number into Network Interface

Correct Answer: 1

Explanation

You can centrally create, enforce, and log application and network connectivity policies across subscriptions and virtual networks. Azure Firewall uses a static public IP address for your virtual network resources allowing outside firewalls to identify traffic originating from your virtual network.

Ref:

- https://docs.microsoft.com/en-us/azure/firewall/features

Web Application Firewall

29. You need to ensure that virtual machine available on Azure are accessible from the Internet over HTTP. Which of the following should you do to reach this goal ?

1. You modify an Azure firewall.
1. You modify an Azure Traffic Manager profile.
2. You modify a DDoS protection plan.
3. Modify a network security group (NGS)

Correct Answer: 1,4

Explanation

Azure Firewall provides inbound protection for non-HTTP/S protocols (for example, RDP, SSH, FTP), outbound network-level protection for all ports and protocols, and application-level protection for outbound HTTP/S.

REF:

- https://docs.microsoft.com/en-us/azure/web-application-firewall/ag/ag-overview

30. Which Azure service listed provides network traffic filtering across multiple Azure subscriptions, resources groups and virtual networks?

1. Azure Firewall
1. an application security group
2. 'Azure DDoS protection
3. a network security group (NSG)

Correct Answer: 1

Explanation

You can restrict traffic to multiple virtual networks in multiple subscriptions with a single Azure firewall.

Azure Firewall is a managed, cloud-based network security service that protects your Azure Virtual Network resources. It's a fully stateful firewall as a service with built-in high availability and unrestricted cloud scalability.

You can centrally create, enforce, and log application and network connectivity policies across subscriptions and virtual networks. Azure Firewall uses a static public IP address for your virtual network resources allowing outside firewalls to identify traffic originating from your virtual network.

REF:

- https://docs.microsoft.com/en-us/azure/firewall/overview

DDoS Protection

31. You need to configure an Azure solution that secures websites from attacks and generates reports that contain details of attempted attacks. What should you include in the solution?

1. Azure Firewall
1. a network security group (NSG)
2. Azure Information Protection
3. DDoS protection

Correct Answer: 4

Explanation

A DDoS attack attempts to exhaust an application's resources, making the application unavailable to legitimate users. DDoS attacks can be targeted at any endpoint that is publicly reachable through the internet. DDOS Protection Product features include:

- Always-on monitoring and automatic network attack mitigation
- Adaptive tuning based on platform insights in Azure
- Application layer protection with Azure Application Gateway Web Application Firewall
- Integration with Azure Monitor for analytics and insights
- Protection against the unforeseen costs of a DDoS attack

Ref:

- https://docs.microsoft.com/en-us/azure/ddos-protection/ddos-protection-overview

32. What kind of Attack is it called when hackers flood the bandwidth or resources of a targeted system, usually one or more web servers using more than one unique IP address or machines, often from thousands of hosts infected with malware?

1. Distributed Denial of Service Attack
   1. Cross-Site Scripting Attack
   2. Man-In-the-Middle Attack
   3. SQL Injection Attack

Correct Answer: 1

Explanation

A distributed denial of service attack attempts to overwhelm and exhaust an application's resources, making the application slow or unresponsive to legitimate users. DDoS attacks can target any resource that's publicly reachable through the internet, including websites.

Ref:

- https://docs.microsoft.com/en-us/learn/modules/secure-network-connectivity-azure/4-protect-attacks-azure-ddos-protection

33. An attacker can bring down your website by sending a large volume of network traffic to your servers. Which Azure service can help Tailwind Traders protect its App Service instance from this kind of attack?

1. Azure Firewall
   1. Network security groups
   2. Azure DDoS Protection

Correct Answer: 3

Explanation

DDoS Protection helps protect your Azure resources from DDoS attacks. A DDoS attack attempts to overwhelm and exhaust an application's resources, making the application slow or unresponsive to legitimate users.

Ref:

- https://docs.microsoft.com/en-us/learn/modules/secure-network-connectivity-azure/4-protect-attacks-azure-ddos-protection

Defense in depth

34. The following are Layers of Defense in depth in Azure. Which one of them is not a layer under Defense in depth?

1. Network Layer
1. Data Layer
2. Webapp layer
3. Compute Layer
4. Perimeter Layer

Correct Answer: 3

Explanation

Defense in depth has the following layers:

- The physical security layer is the first line of defense to protect computing hardware in the datacenter
  - The identity and access layer controls access to infrastructure and change control.
  - The perimeter layer uses distributed denial of service (DDoS) protection to filter large-scale attacks before they can cause a denial of service for users.
- The network layer limits communication between resources through segmentation and access controls.
  - The compute layer secures access to virtual machines.
  - The application layer helps ensure that applications are secure and free of security vulnerabilities.
- The data layer controls access to business and customer data that you need to protect.

Ref:

- https://docs.microsoft.com/en-us/learn/modules/secure-network-connectivity-azure/2-what-is-defense-in-depth

35. What does security posture mean to your company in relation to Azure?

1. Ability to control your data movement across Azure
1. Ability to protect from and respond to security threats
2. Ability to ensure data is available to everyone in company securely
3. Ability to deal with security breaches on Azure

Correct Answer: 2

Explanation

Your security posture is your organization's ability to protect from and respond to security threats. The common principles used to define a security posture are confidentiality, integrity, and availability, known collectively as CIA.

Ref:

- https://docs.microsoft.com/en-us/learn/modules/secure-network-connectivity-azure/2-what-is-defense-in-depth

36. When should you ensure your company's, data is secured to prevent unauthorised access and changes as per integrity guidelines under defense in depth?

1. At rest
1. In Azure Storage
2. In transit
3. None of the above

Correct Answer: 1,3

Explanation

To prevent unauthorized access and changes to information, data should be secured when:

- **At rest:** when it's stored.

- **In transit:** when it's being transferred from one place to another, including from a local computer to the cloud. A common approach used in data transmission is for the sender to create a unique fingerprint of the data by using a one-way hashing algorithm. The hash is sent to the receiver along with the data. The receiver recalculates the data's hash and compares it to the original to ensure that the data wasn't lost or modified in transit.

Ref:

- https://docs.microsoft.com/en-us/learn/modules/secure-network-connectivity-azure/2-what-is-defense-in-depth

Application Gateway

37. Your organization is operating with three Availability Zones (AZ). It is decided to deploy multiple instances of a web application across all three AZs. An Azure networking product is then configured by the organization so the service requests can be evenly distributed across all the three instances. Can you identify the Azure networking product that will be used?

1. Content delivery network
1. Application Gateway
2. Load Balancer
3. Web Application firewall

Correct Answer: 2

Explanation

Azure Application Gateway is a web traffic load balancer that enables you to manage traffic to your web applications. Traditional load balancers operate at the transport layer (OSI layer 4 - TCP and UDP) and route traffic based on source IP address and port, to a destination IP address and port

Ref:

- https://docs.microsoft.com/en-us/azure/application-gateway/overview

38. You are troubleshooting a performance issue for an Azure Application Gateway and need to compare the total requests to the failed requests in the last six hours. What should you use?

1. NSG flow logs in Azure Network Watcher.

1. Metrics in Application Gateway.
2. Connection monitor in Azure Network Watcher.
3. Diagnostics logs in Application Gateway.

Correct Answer: 2

Explanation

Application Gateway publishes data points, called metrics, to Azure Monitor for the performance of your Application Gateway and backend instances. These metrics are numerical values in an ordered set of time-series data that describe some aspect of your application gateway at a particular time.

Ref:

- https://docs.microsoft.com/en-us/azure/application-gateway/application-gateway-metrics#:~:text=Application%20Gateway%20publishes%20data%20points,gateway%20at%20a%20particular%20time

Azure Load Balancer

39. Which of the following statements describes the purpose of load balancer resource?

1. It uses URL-based routing to route web traffic across multiple instances
1. 'It distributes virtual machine traffic evenly across multiple instances
2. 'It delivers internet traffic to the datacenter that is geographically closest to the user.
3. it add or removes virtual machine instances as demand increases

Correct Answer: 2

Explanation

Load Balancer distributes inbound flows that arrive at the load balancer's front end to backend pool instances. These flows are according to configured load balancing rules and health probes. The backend pool instances can be Azure Virtual Machines or instances in a virtual machine scale set.

Ref:

- https://docs.microsoft.com/en-us/azure/load-balancer/load-balancer-overview

Azure Monitor Autoscale

40. Autoscaling is used by an Azure Service to add or remove resources. The purpose is to minimize costs and bring in optimum performance levels. Can you identify which of the following Azure Service uses autoscaling?

1. Azure Service Health
1. 'Azure Security Center
2. 'Azure Monitor
3. Azure Advisor

Correct Answer: 3

Explanation

Azure Monitor autoscale provide a common set of autoscaling functionality for virtual machine scale sets, Azure App Service, and Azure Cloud Service. Scaling can be performed on a schedule, or based on a runtime metric, such as CPU or memory usage.

Ref:

- https://docs.microsoft.com/en-us/azure/azure-monitor/platform/autoscale-overview

Security Score

41. What happens when you implement the security recommendations provided by Azure Advisor, your company?s secure score will ?

    1. Your company?s secure score will decrease.

    1. Your company?s secure score will increase.

    2. Your company?s secure score remains the same since it is your obligation.

Correct Answer: 2

Explanation

To increase your security, review Security Center's recommendations page for the outstanding actions necessary to raise your score. Each recommendation includes instructions to help you remediate the specific issues.

Ref:

- https://docs.microsoft.com/en-us/azure/security-center/secure-score-security-controls

Virtual Machines

42. Does Azure virtual machines that run Windows Server 2019 can encrypt the network traffic sent from the virtual machines to a host on the Internet.

1. Yes
1. No

Correct Answer: 2

Explanation

The question is rather vague as it would depend on the configuration of the host on the Internet. Windows Server does come with a VPN client and it also supports other encryption methods such IPSec encryption or SSL/TLS so it could encrypt the traffic if the Internet host was configured to require or accept the encryption. However, the VM could not encrypt the traffic to an Internet host that is not configured to require the encryption.

Ref:

- https://docs.microsoft.com/en-us/azure/virtual-machines/windows/disk-encryption-overview

43. You have an Azure subscription that contains three virtual networks named VNet1, VNet2, and VNet3. VNet2 contains a virtual appliance named VM2 that operates as a router. You are configuring the virtual networks in a hub and spoke topology that uses VNet2 as the hub network. You plan to configure peering between VNet1 and Vnet2 and between VNet2 and VNet3. You need to provide connectivity between VNet1 and VNet3 through VNet2. Which two configurations should you perform?

1. On the peering connections, use remote gateways.
1. B. On the peering connections, allow forwarded traffic.
2. C. On the peering connections, allow gateway transit.
3. D. Create route tables and assign the table to subnets.
4. E. Create a route filter.

Correct Answer: 1,3

Explanation

Allow gateway transit: Check this box if you have a virtual network gateway attached to this virtual network and want to allow traffic from the peered virtual network to flow through the gateway. For example, this virtual network may be attached to an on-premises network through a virtual network gateway. The gateway can be an ExpressRoute or VPN gateway. Checking this box allows traffic from the peered virtual network to flow through the gateway attached to this virtual network to the on-premises network.

If you check this box, the peered virtual network cannot have a gateway configured. The peered virtual network must have the Use remote gateways checkbox checked when setting up the peering from the other virtual network to this virtual network. If you leave this box unchecked (default), traffic from the peered virtual network still flows to this virtual network, but cannot flow through a virtual network gateway attached to this virtual network. If the peering is between a virtual network (Resource Manager) and a virtual network (classic), the gateway must be in the virtual network (Resource Manager).

Ref:

- https://docs.microsoft.com/en-us/azure/virtual-network/virtual-network-peering-overview

44. You have an Azure subscription that contains the following resources:
i) Name: VNet1, Type: virtual network, Azure region: West US, Resource group: RG2
ii) Name: VNet2, Type: virtual network, Azure region: West US. Resource group: RG1
iii) Name: VNet3, Type: virtual network, Azure region: East US, Resource group: RG1
iv) Name: NSG1, Type: Network security group (NSG)Azure region: East US, Resource group: RG2
To which subnets can you apply NSG1?

1. The subnets on VNet2 only.
1. The subnets on VNet2 and VNet3 only.
2. The subnets on VNet1, VNet2, and VNet3.
3. The subnets on VNet1 only.
4. The subnets on VNet3 only

Correct Answer: 5

Explanation

All Azure resources are created in an Azure region and subscription. A resource can only be created in a virtual network that exists in the same region and subscription as the resource. You can however, connect virtual networks that exist in different subscriptions and regions.

Ref:

- https://docs.microsoft.com/en-us/azure/virtual-network/manage-network-security-group

45. You company?s Azure subscription contains a policy-based virtual network gateway and a virtual network. You need to ensure that you can configure a point-to-site connection from the Virtual network to an on-premises computer.
Which two actions should you perform?

1. Reset GW1.
1. Create a route-based virtual network gateway.
2. Delete GW1.
3. DAdd a public IP address space to VNet1.
4. Add a connection to GW1.
5. Add a service endpoint to VNet1

Correct Answer: 3,2

Explanation

A VPN gateway is used when creating a VPN connection to your on-premises network. Route-based VPN devices use any-to-any (wildcard) traffic selectors, and let routing/forwarding tables direct traffic to different IPsec tunnels. It is typically built on router platforms where each IPsec tunnel is modelled as a network interface or VTI (virtual tunnel interface). Policy-based VPN devices use the combinations of prefixes from both networks to define how traffic is encrypted/decrypted through IPsec tunnels. It is typically built on firewall devices that perform packet filtering. IPsec tunnel encryption and decryption are added to the packet filtering and processing engine. Point-to-Site connections do not require a VPN device or a public-facing IP address.

46. You company Azure environment contains multiple Azure virtual machines. You plan to implement a solution that enables the client computers on your on-premises network to communicate to the Azure VMs. Which Azure resources must be created for the planned solution?

1. ' A virtual network gateway.
1. A load balancer.
2. An application gateway.
3. A virtual network.
4. A gateway subnet.

Correct Answer: 4,5

Explanation

A VPN gateway is a specific type of virtual network gateway that is used to send encrypted traffic between an Azure virtual network and an on-premises location over the public Internet. You can also use a VPN gateway to send encrypted traffic between Azure virtual networks over the Microsoft network. Each virtual network can have only one VPN gateway. However, you can create multiple connections to the same VPN gateway. When you create multiple connections to the same VPN gateway, all VPN tunnels share the available gateway bandwidth.

Ref:

- https://docs.microsoft.com/en-us/azure/vpn-gateway/vpn-gateway-about-vpngateways

47. Which of the following address block/range CANNOT be used in an Azure Virtual Network?

1. 10.0.0.0 - 10.255.255.255
1. 172.16.0.0 - 172.31.255.255
2. 192.168.0.0 - 192.168.255.255
3. 127.0.0.0 ? 127.0.0.255

Correct Answer: 4

Explanation

Address 127.0.0.0 is used for loopback or localhost. Azure recommend that you use the address ranges enumerated in RFC 1918, which have been set aside by the IETF for private, non-routable address spaces:

- 10.0.0.0 - 10.255.255.255 (10/8 prefix)
- 172.16.0.0 - 172.31.255.255 (172.16/12 prefix)
- 192.168.0.0 - 192.168.255.255 (192.168/16 prefix)

In addition, you cannot add the following address ranges:

- 224.0.0.0/4 (Multicast)
- 255.255.255.255/32 (Broadcast)
- 127.0.0.0/8 (Loopback)
- 169.254.0.0/16 (Link-local)
- 168.63.129.16/32 (Internal DNS)

Ref:

- https://docs.microsoft.com/en-us/azure/virtual-network/virtual-networks-faq

48. Which of the following tasks would you NOT be able to perform to a Subnet or Virtual Network once it has been created?

1. Add new Subnets to a Virtual Network already deployed.
1. Add CIDR block to Virtual Network already deployed.
2. Modify the size of subnet after creating it.
3. Use tracert to diagnose connectivity issues.
4. Ping your routers within the Virtual Network.

Correct Answer: 4,5

Explanation

Subnets can be added to VNets at any time as long as the subnet address range is not part of another subnet and there is available space left in the virtual network's address range. You can add, remove, expand, or shrink a subnet if there are no VMs or services deployed within it. You can add, remove, and modify the CIDR blocks used by a VNet.

Ref:

- https://docs.microsoft.com/en-us/azure/virtual-network/virtual-networks-faq

Load Balancer

49. You have a public load balancer that balances ports 80 and 443 across three virtual machines. You need to direct all the Remote Desktop Protocol (RDP) connections to VM3 only. What should you configure?

1. An inbound NAT rule.
1. A load balancing rule.
2. A new public load balancer for VM3.
3. A frontend IP configuration.

Correct Answer: 1

Explanation

Create an inbound NAT port-forwarding rule: Create a load balancer inbound network address translation (NAT) rule to forward traffic from a specific port of the front-end IP address to a specific port of a back-end VM.

Ref:

- https://docs.microsoft.com/en-us/azure/load-balancer/tutorial-load-balancer-port-forwarding-portal

50. You have five Azure virtual configured as web servers and an Azure load balancer that provides load balancing services for the virtual machines. You need to ensure that visitors are serviced by the same web server for each request. What should you configure?

1. Protocol to UDP.
1. Session persistence to None.
2. Session persistence to Client IP.
3. dle Time-out (minutes) to 20.

Correct Answer: 3

Explanation

Session persistence to Client IP. You can set the sticky session in load balancer rules with setting the session persistence as the client IP address.

Ref:

- https://docs.microsoft.com/en-us/azure/load-balancer/load-balancer-distribution-mode

PART 6

Describe identity governance privacy and compliance features

Azure Active directory

1. The process of proving you are who you say you are is called?

1. Authorization
1. Authentication
2. Validation
3. Login

Correct Answer: 2

Explanation

> Authentication is the process of proving you are who you say you are. Authentication is sometimes shortened to AuthN. Microsoft identity platform implements the OpenID Connect protocol for handling authentication.

Ref:

- https://docs.microsoft.com/en-us/azure/active-directory/develop/authentication-vs-authorization

2. The act of granting an allowed party permission to do something is called?

1. Authorization
1. Authentication
2. Validation
3. Login

Correct Answer: 1

Explanation

Authorization is the act of granting an authenticated party permission to do something. It specifies what data you're allowed to access and what you can do with that data. Authorization is sometimes shortened to AuthZ. Microsoft identity platform implements the OAuth 2.0 protocol for handling authorization.

Ref:

- https://docs.microsoft.com/en-us/azure/active-directory/develop/authentication-vs-authorization

3. You need to ensure that when Azure Active Directory (Azure AD) users connect to Azure AD from the Internet by using an anonymous IP address, the users are prompted automatically to change their password. Which Azure service should you use?

1. Azure AD Connect Health
1. Azure AD Privileged Identity Management
2. Azure Advanced Threat Protection (ATP)
3. Azure AD Identity Protection

Correct Answer: 4

Explanation

Azure Active Directory Identity Protection enables organizations to configure automated responses to detected suspicious actions related to user identities.

Microsoft has secured cloud-based identities for more than a decade. With Azure Active Directory Identity Protection, in your environment, you can use the same protection systems Microsoft uses to secure identities.

Ref:

- https://docs.microsoft.com/en-us/azure/active-directory/identity-protection/overview-identity-protection

4. Your Company wants to develop and deploy some WebApps, for which it subscribes to Azure as a platform. It is desired to keep the expenses to a minimum before the app is finally released. You have to identify the features available in Azure Active Directory (AD) Free edition. Choose two options from below that are available in the Azure Active Directory (AD) Free edition.

1. Company branding
1. User and Group management
2. 'Group based access management
3. Self-service password Change for cloud users

Correct Answer: 2,4

Explanation

Azure AD free offers:

- Limited to 500,000 Directory Objects.
- Identity management capabilities and device registration.
- Single Sign-On can be assigned to 10 apps per user.
- B2B collaboration capabilities (allows you to assign guest users that exist outside of your business).
- Self-service password change (cloud users)
- Connect (syncs on-premise AD to Azure AD)
- Basic security reports.

Ref:

- https://azure.microsoft.com/en-us/trial/get-started-active-directory/

5. The following are services provided by Azure Active Directory. Which of the given options is NOT an Azure Ad service?

1. Authentication
1. Single sign-on
2. Threat detection
3. Device management

Correct Answer: 1

Explanation

Azure AD provides services such as:

- **Authentication:** This includes verifying identity to access applications and resources.
- **Single sign-on:** SSO enables you to remember only one username and one password to access multiple applications.
- **Application management:** You can manage your cloud and on-premises apps by using Azure AD.
- **Device management:** Along with accounts for individual people, Azure AD supports the registration of devices.

Ref:

- https://docs.microsoft.com/en-us/learn/modules/secure-access-azure-identity-services/3-what-is-azure-active-directory

6. Azure AD Connect synchronizes user identities between which two main Directory?

1. Azure AD and windows Virtual Machines
1. Azure Ad and Single sign-on
2. Azure AD and Active Directory
3. Azure AD and Azure AuthZ

Explanation

Azure AD Connect synchronizes user identities between on-premises Active Directory and Azure AD. Azure AD Connect synchronizes changes between both identity systems, so you can use features like SSO, multifactor authentication, and self-service password reset under both systems. Self-service password reset prevents users from using known compromised passwords.

Ref:

- https://docs.microsoft.com/en-us/azure/architecture/reference-architectures/identity/azure-ad

7. What is an Instance of Azure AD created by your organization and acts as a directory service for cloud applications by storing objects copied from the on-premises Active Directory and provides identity services called?

1. Azure AD connect
1. Azure AD tenant
2. Azure Domain
3. Active Directory

Correct Answer: 2

Explanation

A tenant is a representation of an organization. It's a dedicated instance of Azure AD that an organization or app developer receives when the organization or app developer creates a relationship with Microsoft-- like signing up for Azure, Microsoft Intune, or Microsoft 365.

Ref:

- https://docs.microsoft.com/en-us/azure/active-directory/develop/quickstart-create-new-tenant

8. Which of the following statements are true?

1. Identities stored in an on-premises Active Directory can be synchronized to Azure Active Directory (Azure AD).
1. Identities stored in Azure Active Directory (Azure AD), third-party cloud services, and on-premises Active Directory can be used to access Azure resources.
2. Azure has built-in authentication and authorization services that provide secure access to Azure resources.

Correct Answer: 1,3

Explanation

By default, on-premise AD and Azure AD are not synced but can be synced when needed. Option B: states that identities store in on-premises Active Directory can also be used to access Azure resources. Identities in On-premise Active Directories have to be brought into Azure AD via AD connect.

Ref:

- https://docs.microsoft.com/en-us/azure/architecture/reference-architectures/identity/azure-ad

9. Which of the following statements is true about Azure AD?

1. Azure Active Directory (Azure AD) requires the implementation of domain controllers on Azure virtual machines.
1. Azure Active Directory (Azure AD) provides authentication services for resources hosted in Azure and Microsoft 365.

2. Each user account in Azure Active Directory (Azure AD) can be assigned only one license.

Correct Answer: 2

Explanation

Azure AD provides authentication services for resources hosted in Azure and Microsoft 365 resources loke Office365 etc.

Ref:

- https://docs.microsoft.com/en-us/azure/architecture/reference-architectures/identity/azure-ad

10. Is it possible to have multiple Global Administrators in Azure AD tenant?

1. Yes
1. No

Correct Answer: 1

Explanation

You can have multiple Global administrators, but only Global administrators can assign administrator roles (including assigning other Global administrators) to users. Note that this administrator role is called Global administrator in the Azure portal, but it's called Company administrator in the Microsoft Graph API and Azure AD PowerShell.

Ref:

- https://docs.microsoft.com/en-us/azure/active-directory/roles/permissions-reference

Privacy Statement

11. What explains what data Microsoft processes, how Microsoft processes the data, and the purpose of processing the data?

1. Microsoft Privacy Statement.
1. Microsoft Online Services Terms
2. Microsoft Online Service Level Agreement
3. Online Subscription Agreement for Microsoft Azure

Correct Answer: 1

Explanation

The Microsoft Privacy Statement explains what personal data Microsoft processes, how Microsoft processes the data, and the purpose of processing the data.

Ref:

- https://privacy.microsoft.com/en-us/privacystatement

Azure Accounts

12. Your Azure trial account expired last week. Which of the following task that you CANNOT perform in Azure?

1. create additional Azure Active Directory (Azure AD) user accounts.
1. start an existing Azure virtual machine
2. access your data stored in Azure
3. access the Azure portal

Correct Answer: 2

Explanation

start an existing Azure virtual machine. A stopped (deallocated) VM is offline and not mounted on an Azure host server. Starting a VM mounts the VM on a host server before the VM starts. As soon as the VM is mounted, it becomes chargeable. For this reason, you are unable to start a VM after a trial has expired.

Ref:

- https://azure.microsoft.com/en-us/resources/knowledge-center/what-happens-when-my-azure-trial-expires/

Azure Policy

13. You have an Azure virtual network named VN1 in a resource group named ReG. You assign an Azure Policy definition of Not Allowed Resource Type and specify that virtual networks are not an allowed resource type in ReG. What will happen to VN?

1. VN is deleted automatically
1. is moved automatically to another resource group
2. continues to function normally
3. is now a read-only object

Correct Answer: 3

Explanation

VN continues to function normally. While these effects primarily affect a resource when the resource is created or updated, Azure Policy also supports dealing with existing non-compliant resources without needing to alter that resource.

Ref:

- https://docs.microsoft.com/en-us/azure/governance/policy/concepts/effects

14. Which of the following describes the role played by Azure policy?

1. Enables you to create, assign, and manage policies that control or audit your resources.
1. Monitor maximizes the availability and performance of your applications by delivering a comprehensive solution for collecting, analysing, and acting on telemetry from your cloud and on-premises environments

2. Displays personalized recommendations for all your subscriptions

Correct Answer: 1

Explanation

Azure Policy is a service in Azure that enables you to create, assign, and manage policies that control or audit your resources. These policies enforce different rules and effects over your resource configurations so that those configurations stay compliant with corporate standards.

15. You have a resource group that you need to use only for storage account. You need to prevent your workmates from creating all other resources in that resource group. What do you need?

1. A lock
1. an Azure role
2. 'a tag
3. an Azure policy

Correct Answer: 4

Explanation

An Azure policy can be assigned ..It can be assigned within a specific scope. This scope could range from a management group to an individual resource. The term scope refers to all the resources, resource groups, subscriptions, or management groups that the policy definition is assigned to. A lock will prevent creation of more resources including the storage accounts.

REF:

- https://docs.microsoft.com/en-us/azure/azure-resource-manager/resource-group-lock-resources

16. Which is the best way for your company to ensure that the team deploys only cost-effective virtual machine SKU sizes?

1. Create a policy in Azure Policy that specifies the allowed SKU sizes.
1. Periodically inspect the deployment manually to see which SKU sizes are used.
2. Create an Azure RBAC role that defines the allowed virtual machine SKU sizes.

Correct Answer: 1

Explanation

After you enable this policy, that policy is applied when you create new virtual machines or resize existing ones. Azure Policy also evaluates any current virtual machines in your environment.

Ref:

- https://docs.microsoft.com/en-us/azure/governance/policy/overview

Azure Role-based Acess (RBAC)

17. A new policy has been implemented in your organization that limits access to resource group and resource scopes in a detailed, granular way. Various groups and users will be provided access. What would you choose to use if you want to implement the new policy?

1. Azure Advisor
1. Role-based access control (RBAC)
2. Azure Policies
3. Locks

Correct Answer: 2

Explanation

Azure role-based access control (Azure RBAC) helps you manage who has access to Azure resources, what they can do with those resources, and what areas they have access to. Azure RBAC is an authorization system built on Azure Resource Manager that provides fine-grained access management of Azure resources.

Ref:

- https://docs.microsoft.com/en-us/azure/role-based-access-control/overview

18. Describe what Azure Role-Based Access Control is.

1. enables you to remember only one username and one password to access multiple applications.
1. process where a user is prompted during the sign-in process for an additional form of identification

2. practice to grant users only the rights they need to perform their job, and only to the relevant resources.
3. process of designing roles to your IT department team

Correct Answer: 3

Explanation

Azure role-based access control (Azure RBAC) helps you manage who has access to Azure resources, what they can do with those resources, and what areas they have access to. Azure RBAC is an authorization system built on Azure Resource Manager that provides fine-grained access management of Azure resources.

Ref:

- https://docs.microsoft.com/en-us/azure/role-based-access-control/overview

19. According to RBAC, what is the name given to the process of attaching a role definition to a user, group, service principal, or managed identity at a particular scope for the purpose of granting access

1. Management role
1. Role assignment
2. Access control
3. role administration

Correct Answer: 2

Explanation

A role assignment is the process of attaching a role definition to a user, group, service principal, or managed identity at a particular scope for the purpose of granting access. Access is granted by creating a role assignment, and access is revoked by removing a role assignment. You can create role assignments using the Azure portal, Azure CLI, Azure PowerShell, Azure SDKs, or REST APIs.

20. How can your company allow some users to control the virtual machines in each environment but prevent them from modifying networking and other resources in the same resource group or Azure subscription?

1. Create a role assignment through Azure role-based access control (Azure RBAC).
1. Create a policy in Azure Policy that audits resource usage.
2. Split the environment into separate resource groups.

Correct Answer: 1

Explanation

Azure RBAC enables you to create roles that define access permissions. You might create one role that limits access only to virtual machines and a second role that provides administrators with access to everything

21. A new policy has been implemented in your organization that limits access to resource group and resource scopes in a detailed, granular way. Various groups and users will be provided access. What would you choose to use if you want to implement the new policy?

1. Azure Advisor
1. Role-based access control (RBAC)
2. Azure Policies
3. 'Locks

Explanation

Azure RBAC is an authorization system built on Azure Resource Manager that provides fine-grained access management of Azure resources.

Ref:

- https://docs.microsoft.com/en-us/azure/role-based-access-control/overview

22 .Service Administrator role enables you to manage all Azure resources, including access. Which of the following roles listed below has the same scope as that of service Admin?

1. Azure Global Administrator
1. Azure Account Administrator
2. Owner Role
3. Azure tenant

Correct Answer: 3

Explanation

Owner role helps you manage all Azure resources, including access. This role is built on a newer authorization system called Azure role-base access control (Azure RBAC) that provides fine-grained access management to Azure resources.

Ref:

- https://docs.microsoft.com/en-us/azure/role-based-access-control/rbac-and-directory-admin-roles

23. Which of the following roles are not performed by the Azure Account Administrator holder?

1. Manage billing in the'Azure portal
1. Create resource locks

2. Manage all subscriptions in an account
3. Create new subscriptions
4. Choose the Global Administrators in Azure AD

Correct Answer: 2,5

Explanation

Account Administrator role is conceptually the billing owner of the subscription. Their roles include:

- Manage billing in the Azure portal
- Manage all subscriptions in an account
  - Create new subscriptions
    - Cancel subscriptions
  - Change the billing for a subscription
    - Change the Service Administrator

Ref:

- https://docs.microsoft.com/en-us/azure/role-based-access-control/rbac-and-directory-admin-roles

24. Which of the following tasks can someone assigned Contributor role in RBAC NOT perform?

1. Create and manage all of types of Azure resources
1. Create a new tenant in Azure Active Directory
2. Grant access to others
3. View all Azure resources

Correct Answer: 3

Explanation

Contributor role has full access to manage all resources, but does not allow you to assign roles in Azure RBAC, manage assignments in Azure Blueprints, or share image galleries.

Ref:

- https://docs.microsoft.com/en-us/azure/role-based-access-control/built-in-roles

Azure Advanced Threat Protection (ATP)

25. You plan to implement several security services for an Azure environment. You need to identify which Azure services must be used to meet the following security requirements:
Monitor threats by using sensors
Enforce Azure Multi-Factor Authentication (MFA) based on a condition
Which Azure service should you identify for each requirement?

1. Azure Monitor
1. Azure Security Center
2. Azure Active Directory (Azure AD) Identity Protection
3. Azure Advanced Threat Protection (ATP)

Correct Answer: 4

Explanation

Azure Advanced Threat Protection (ATP): Monitor threats by using sensors. Azure Advanced Threat Protection (ATP) is a cloud-based security solution that leverages your on-premises Active Directory signals to identify, detect, and investigate advanced threats, compromised identities, and malicious insider actions directed at your organization. Sensors are software packages you install on your servers to upload information to Azure ATP.

Azure Active Directory (Azure AD) Identity Protection: Enforce Azure Multi-Factor Authentication (MFA) based on a condition. Azure AD Identity Protection helps you manage the roll-out of Azure Multi-Factor Authentication (MFA) registration by configuring a Conditional Access policy to require MFA registration no matter what modern authentication app you are signing in to.

Ref:

- https://docs.microsoft.com/en-us/defender-for-identity/what-is

Single Sign- on

26. What is Single sign-on on Azure Active Directory?

1. Enables just one password for all your resources.
1. enables you to remember only one username and one password to access multiple applications.
2. Enables you to have strong password for all logins.
3. Enables you to log into Azure without a password.

Correct Answer: 2

Explanation

Single sign-on enables a user to sign in one time and use that credential to access multiple resources and applications from different providers. More identities mean more passwords to remember and change. Password policies can vary among applications. As complexity requirements increase, it becomes increasingly difficult for users to remember them. The more passwords a user has to manage, the greater the risk of a credential-related security incident.

Ref:

- https://docs.microsoft.com/en-us/azure/active-directory/manage-apps/what-is-single-sign-on

27. Your company hosts multiple application that workers use for day-to-day work. The workers complain that the number of times they are required to use authenticate into those applications is a lot. How can the IT department reduce the number of times users must authenticate to access multiple applications?

1. Azure Multifactor Authentication
1. Azure Single Sign-on

2. Azure AD tenant

3. Azure Conditional Access

Correct Answer: 2

Explanation

Single sign-on enables a user to sign in one time and use that credential to access multiple resources and applications from different providers. More identities mean more passwords to remember and change. Password policies can vary among applications. As complexity requirements increase, it becomes increasingly difficult for users to remember them. The more passwords a user has to manage, the greater the risk of a credential-related security incident.

Ref:

- https://docs.microsoft.com/en-us/azure/active-directory/manage-apps/what-is-single-sign-on

Azure Multifactor Authentication (MFA)

28. What is Azure's Multifactor Authentication (MFA)?

1. process where a user is prompted during the sign-in process for an additional form of identification.
1. enables you to remember only one username and one password to access multiple applications.
2. verifying identity to access applications and resources.
3. Cloud-based security solution that leverages your on-premises Active Directory signals to identify, detect, and investigate compromised identities, and malicious insider actions directed at your organization.

Correct Answer: 1

Explanation

Multifactor authentication is a process where a user is prompted during the sign-in process for an additional form of identification. Examples include a code on their mobile phone or a fingerprint scan.

Ref:

- https://docs.microsoft.com/en-us/azure/active-directory/authentication/concept-mfa-howitworks

29. Multifactor authentication (MFA) provides additional security for your identities by requiring two or more elements to fully authenticate. These elements fall into three categories. Which of the following is NOT in MFA category?

1. Something the user know

1. Something the user is
2. Something the user does
3. Something the use has

Correct Answer: 3

Explanation

MFA maybe categorised into:

- **Something the user knows:** This might be an email address and password.
- **Something the user has:** This might be a code that's sent to the user's mobile phone.
  - **Something the user is:** This is typically some sort of biometric property, such as a fingerprint or face scan that's used on many mobile devices.

Ref:

- https://docs.microsoft.com/en-us/learn/modules/secure-access-azure-identity-services/4-what-are-mfa-conditional-access

30. How can your company's IT department use biometric properties, such as facial recognition, to enable delivery drivers to prove their identities when using company resources and applications?

1. Azure Single Sign-on
1. Azure Active Directory
2. Azure Conditional Access
3. Multifactor authentication

Correct Answer: 4

Explanation

Authenticating through multifactor authentication can include something the user knows, something the user has, and something the user is. Facial recognition and fingerprint are some of examples of MFA something the user is.

Ref:

- https://docs.microsoft.com/en-us/azure/active-directory/authentication/concept-mfa-howitworks

31. In what way does Multi-Factor Authentication increase the security of a user account?

1. It requires the user to possess something like their phone to read an SMS or use a mobile app or provide a fingerprint or other biometric identification
1. It requires users to provide a very strong password
2. It requires users to be approved before they can log in for the first time.
3. It doesn't. Multi-Factor Authentication is more about access and authentication than account security

Correct Answer: 1

Explanation

Multifactor authentication (MFA) provides additional security for your identities by requiring two or more elements to fully authenticate a user in addition to a password.

Ref:

- https://docs.microsoft.com/en-us/azure/active-directory/authentication/concept-mfa-howitworks

Azure Advanced Threat Protection (ATP)

32. Describe what is Azure Advanced Threat Protection service.

1. enables you to remember only one username and one password to access multiple applications.
1. process where a user is prompted during the sign-in process for an additional form of identification.
2. verifying identity to access applications and resources.
3. Cloud-based security solution that leverages your on-premises Active Directory signals to identify, detect, and investigate compromised identities, and malicious insider actions directed at your organization.

Correct Answer: 4

Explanation

Azure ATP gathers information to help protect the system. This means gathering signals and sending that information into Azure. If someone is logging in from multiple access points, it can submit that information. Azure ATP collects signals that may otherwise be considered suspicious for further evaluation or consideration. Because Azure ATP is able to collect information about patterns and traffic, it can pass all these signals along, notifying someone when a collection of signals come up. It can also relay specific information such as what the issue was or how it should be hunted down.

Ref:

- https://docs.microsoft.com/en-us/azure/security/fundamentals/threat-detection

Azure Conditional Access

33. Which of the following tool that Azure Active Directory uses to allow (or deny) access to resources based on identity signals?

1. Azure AD tenant
1. Azure Multifactor Authentication
2. Conditional Access
3. Single sign-on

Correct Answer: 3

Explanation

Conditional Access is a tool that Azure Active Directory uses to allow (or deny) access to resources based on identity signals. These signals include who the user is, where the user is, and what device the user is requesting access from.

Ref:

- https://docs.microsoft.com/en-us/azure/active-directory/conditional-access/overview

34. Conditional Access comes with a decision-making tool that helps Azure resource administrator plan and troubleshoot your Conditional Access policies. What's the name of this tool?

1. Else if tool
1. What if tool
2. while tool
3. Do this tool

Correct Answer: 2

Explanation

> The Azure AD conditional access What if tool allows you to understand the impact of your conditional access policies on your environment. Instead of test driving your policies by performing multiple sign-ins manually, this tool enables you to evaluate a simulated sign-in of a user.

Ref:

- https://azure.microsoft.com/en-us/updates/azure-ad-conditional-access-what-if-tool-is-now-available

35. Your company has Hybrid Cloud structure with some of the resources hosted in Azure. As the IT administrator, how do you ensure that employees at the company's access company applications hosted in Azure only from approved laptop devices?

1. Azure Multifactor Authentication
1. Azure Single Sign-on
2. Azure AD tenant
3. Azure Conditional Access

Correct Answer: 4

Explanation

Conditional Access enables you to require users to access your applications only from approved, or managed, devices. Conditional Access is a tool that Azure Active Directory uses to allow (or deny) access to resources based on identity signals. These signals include who the user is, where the user is, and what device the user is requesting access from.

Ref:

- https://docs.microsoft.com/en-us/azure/active-directory/conditional-access/overview

Resources Lock

36. You have created a VM in resource group in Azure Resources manager. You need to prevent anyone from ever deleting the VM since it contains some important testing files. Which of following policies should you use?

1. Read Lock
1. Delete Lock
2. Write Lock
3. Read-only lock
4. Resource Lock

Correct Answer: 2

Explanation

here are two types of resource locks. one, Read-only lock that allows to check resources but do not allow any changes. Two, delete lock that allows to change resources except delete. This is to protect resources from accidental/unwanted deletes. so it requires Delete lock at the resource group level. If the Delete lock is at subscription level then that inherits to RG under the subscription. To answer question, it's Delete Lock and not generally resource lock.

REF:

- https://docs.microsoft.com/en-us/azure/governance/blueprints/concepts/resource-locking

37. What level of locking are available for Azure resources?

1. Delete Locks
1. Read only locks
2. Deploy locks

3. Authorization lock

Correct Answer: 1,2

Explanation

You can set the lock level to Delete or Read-only.

- **Delete** means authorized people can still read and modify a resource, but they can't delete the resource without first removing the lock.
- **Read-only** means authorized people can read a resource, but they can't delete or change the resource. Applying this lock is like restricting all authorized users to the permissions granted by the Reader role in Azure RBAC.

Ref:

- https://docs.microsoft.com/en-us/azure/azure-resource-manager/management/lock-resources

Tags

38. You company Azure subscription has a resource group that contains 50 virtual machines and 10 blob storages. Your company has three cost centres named Manufacturing, Sales, and Finance. You need to associate each resource in the resource group to a specific cost centre. What should you do?

1. Configure locks for the virtual machine.
1. Add an extension to the virtual machines.
2. Assign tags to the virtual machines.
3. Modify the inventory settings of the virtual machine

Billing Tags Policy Initiative: Requires specified tag values for cost centre and product name. Uses built-in policies to apply and enforce required tags. You specify the required values for the tags.

Ref:

- https://docs.microsoft.com/en-us/azure/azure-resource-manager/management/tag-resources

39. Which is likely the best way for your company to identify which billing department each Azure resource belongs to?

1. Track resource usage in a spreadsheet.
1. Split the deployment into separate Azure subscriptions, where each subscription belongs to its own billing department.
2. Apply a tag to each resource that includes the associated billing department

Correct Answer: 3

Explanation

Tags provide extra information, or metadata, about your resources. The team might create a tag that's named BillingDept whose value would be the name of the billing department. You can use Azure Policy to ensure that the proper tags are assigned when resources are provisioned.

Ref:

- https://docs.microsoft.com/en-us/azure/azure-resource-manager/management/tag-resource

Azure Blueprints

40. What is the alternative of having Azure policies when you have multiple subscriptions requiring different policies?

1. Azure Monitor
1. Azure Management Groups
2. Azure subscription Locks
3. Azure Blueprints

Correct Answer: 4

Explanation

Instead of having to configure features like Azure Policy for each new subscription, with Azure Blueprints you can define a repeatable set of governance tools and standard Azure resources that your organization requires. In this way, development teams can rapidly build and deploy new environments with the knowledge that they're building within organizational compliance with a set of built-in components that speed the development and deployment phases.

Ref:

- https://docs.microsoft.com/en-us/azure/governance/blueprints/overview

Online Service Terms (OST)

41. legal agreement between Microsoft and the customer that details the obligations by both parties with respect to the processing and security of customer data and personal data is called?

1. Microsoft Privacy statement
1. Microsoft Data statement
2. Online service terms
3. Microsoft Compliance statement

Correct Answer: 3

Explanation

The Online Services Terms (OST) is a legal agreement between Microsoft and the customer. The OST details the obligations by both parties with respect to the processing and security of customer data and personal data. The OST applies specifically to Microsoft's online services that you license through a subscription, including Azure, Dynamics 365, Office 365, and Bing Maps.

Ref:

- https://www.microsoft.com/en-us/microsoft-365/blog/2020/01/08/updated-microsoft-online-services-terms-available-around-world/

Data Protection Addendum (DPA)

42. The Microsoft Data Protection Addendum (DPA) further defines the data processing and security terms for online services. Which of the following is NOT among DPA terms?

1. Compliance with laws.
1. Disclosure of processed data.
2. Data transfer, retention, and deletion.
3. Data exposure to government contractors.

Correct Answer: 4

Explanation

The Data Protection Addendum (DPA) further defines the data processing and security terms for online services. These terms include:

- Compliance with laws.
- Disclosure of processed data.
- Data Security, which includes security practices and policies, data encryption, data access, customer responsibilities, and compliance with auditing.
- Data transfer, retention, and deletion.

Ref:

- https://docs.microsoft.com/en-us/learn/modules/examine-privacy-compliance-data-protection-standards/3-access-microsoft-privacy-statement

Compliance Manager

43. From which Azure blade can you can track your company's regulatory standards and regulations, such as ISO 27001 availability on Azure?

1. Azure Cloud Shell
1. the Microsoft Cloud Partner Portal
2. Compliance Manager
3. the Trust Center

Correct Answer: 3

Explanation

Microsoft Compliance Manager (Preview) is a free workflow-based risk assessment tool that lets you track, assign, and verify regulatory compliance activities related to Microsoft cloud services. Azure Cloud Shell, on the other hand, is an interactive, authenticated, browser-accessible shell for managing Azure resources.

Ref:

- https://docs.microsoft.com/en-us/microsoft-365/compliance/compliance-manager?view=o365-worldwide

Azure Compliance Documentation

44. Describe the purpose of the Azure compliance documentation

1. risk assessment tool that lets you track, assign, and verify regulatory compliance activities related to Microsoft cloud services.
1. legal agreement between Microsoft and the customer on details the obligations by both parties with respect to the processing and security of customer data and personal data.
2. provides you with detailed documentation about legal and regulatory standards and compliance on Azure

Correct Answer: 3

Explanation

Compliance Documentation means specific documents or information including records, reports, observations and verbal responses required to verify compliance with standards by a facility or program.

Ref :

- https://docs.microsoft.com/en-us/learn/modules/examine-privacy-compliance-data-protection-standards/5-access-azure-compliance-documentation

Azure Global Infrstracture

45. Which two types of customers are eligible to use Azure Government to develop a cloud solution?

1. Canadian government contractor.
1. European government contractor.
2. United States government entity.
3. United States government contractor.
4. European government entity.

Correct Answer: 3,4

Explanation

US government agencies or their partners interested in cloud services that meet government security and compliance requirements, can be confident that Microsoft Azure Government provides world-class security, protection, and compliance services.

Azure Government delivers a dedicated cloud enabling government agencies and their partners to transform mission-critical workloads to the cloud. Azure Government services handle data that is subject to certain government regulations and requirements, such as FedRAMP, NIST 800.171 (DIB), ITAR, IRS 1075, DoD L4, and CJIS.

Ref:

- https://azure.microsoft.com/global-infrastructure/government

46. Why is Azure China Operated by 21Vianet, a different entity from Microsoft Azure themselves?

1. Azure did not have capital to invest in China
1. China governance regulations regarding operating Cloud services in their country

2. Existence of other Cloud giants in China like Huawei and Alibaba Cloud
3. Stiff competition from other global public cloud service providers

Correct Answer: 2

Explanation

According to the China Telecommunication Regulation, providers of cloud services, infrastructure as a service (IaaS) and platform as a service (PaaS), must have value-added telecom permits. Only locally registered companies with less than 50 percent foreign investment qualify for these permits. To comply with this regulation, the Azure service in China is operated by 21Vianet, based on the technologies licensed from Microsoft.

Ref:

- https://docs.microsoft.com/en-us/azure/china

Privacy Statement

47. Where can the team access details about the personal data Microsoft processes and how the company processes it, including for Cortana?

1. Microsoft Privacy Statement
1. The Azure compliance documentation
2. Microsoft compliance offerings
3. Microsoft Trust Center

Correct Answer: 1

Explanation

The Microsoft Privacy Statement provides information that's relevant to specific services, including Cortana

Ref:

- https://privacy.microsoft.com/en-us/privacystatement

Trust Center

48. Where can the legal team access information around how the Microsoft cloud helps them secure sensitive data and comply with applicable laws and regulations?

1. Microsoft Privacy Statement
1. Trust Center
2. Online Services Terms
3. Microsoft cloud partner portal

Correct Answer: 2

Explanation

The Trust Center is a great resource for people in your organization who might play a role in security, privacy, and compliance.

Ref:

- https://www.microsoft.com/en-us/trust-center

49. Where can the IT department find reference blueprints that it can apply directly to its Azure subscriptions?

1. Online Services Terms
1. Azure compliance documentation
2. Microsoft Privacy Statement
3. Trust Center

Correct Answer: 2

Explanation

The compliance documentation provides reference blueprints, or policy definitions, for common standards that you can apply to your Azure subscription.

Ref:

- https://www.microsoft.com/en-us/trust-center/compliance/compliance-overview

Azure AD Tenant

50. To whom does the Azure automatically assign the role of Azure AD Global administrator?

1. The IT administrator
1. The company owner
2. To whoever created Azure AD Tenant
3. To whoever created the last subscription on the account

Correct Answer: 3

Explanation

To Whoever created Azure AD tenant > Azure AD Global administrator role is automatically assigned to whomever created the Azure AD tenant. Global administrators can do all of the administrative functions for Azure AD and any services that federate to Azure AD, such as Exchange Online, SharePoint Online, and Skype for Business Online.

Ref:

- https://docs.microsoft.com/en-us/azure/active-directory/fundamentals/active-directory-whatis

GROKKING THE AZURE
FUNDAMENTALS CERTIFICATION

By going through these questions and topic you will not only expand your knowledge but also get ready for your next Azure certification.

Topics Covered Include:

- Account Permissions
- App Services
- Application Gateway
- Availability Zones
- Azure Accounts
- Azure Active Directory
- Service-Level Agreement (SLA)
- Azure Advanced Threat Protection (ATP)
- Azure Advisor
- Support Plans
- Azure Cognitive Services
- Azure Cost Management
- Azure Database
- Azure Firewall
- Azure Global Infrstracture
- Azure Key Vault
- Azure Monitor
- Azure Portal
- Azure Product Status
- Azure Resource Manager
- Azure Role-Based Access (RBAC)
- Cloud Models
- Big Data
- DDOS Protection
- Network Security Group
- Pricing
- Resource Groups
- Virtual Networks